A TROUBLED MIND

By Neil Spencer

First Published in Great Britain in YEAR

Copyright © 2023 Neil Spencer

Some names included have been changed for security or personal reasons. This book has be written as accurately as possible and from my own recollection of events and memories. Any mistakes are due to my own doing, but I would be happy to address in any future work.

The author has asserted their right under the Copyright, Designs and Patent Act 1988 to be identified as the author of this work. This book is a work of fiction and any resemblance to actual persons living or dead, is purely coincidental.

All rights reserved. No part of this publication may be reproduced or transmitted in any form or by any means, electronic or mechanical, including photocopy, recording, or any information storage and retrieval system, without permission in writing from the publisher.

A CIP catalogue record for this book is available from the British Library

Cover Design by Creative Covers

Typesetting by Book Polishers

This book is dedicated to my wife Selina who has been at my side through the good times and the bad.

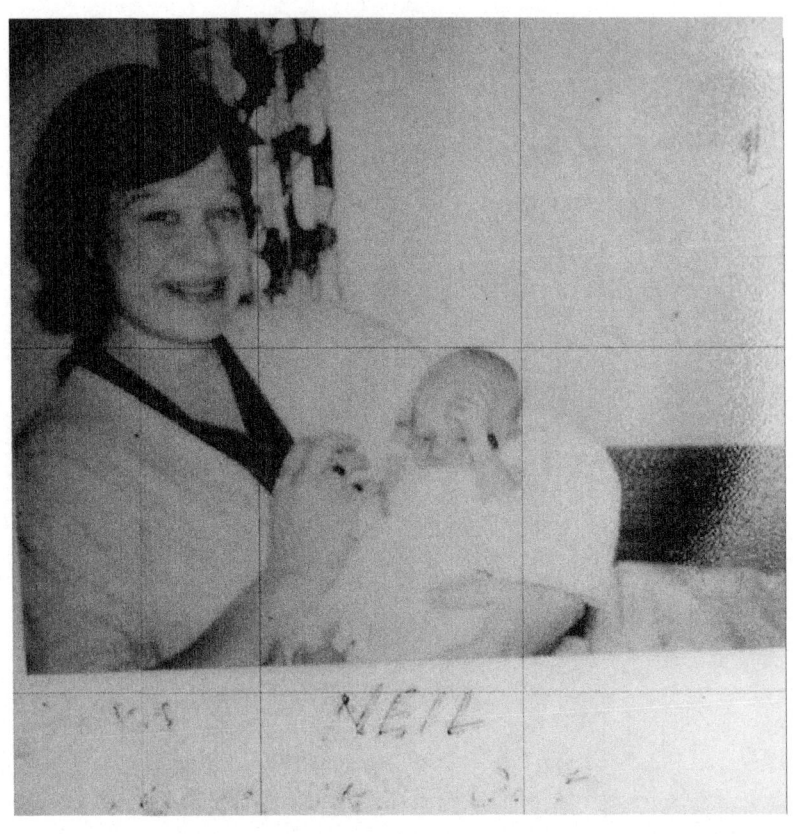

An early photo opportunity with my mother at just 16 hours old.
Even then I had my hands over my head.

Chapter 1

I'm just a delinquent.

IT WAS EARLY 2019 and I was sitting down with my mental health therapist and we were about to try a process called EMDR or Eye movement desensitization and reprocessing. I was asked to focus on the movement of the therapists finger while thinking back to a traumatic time in my life.

I was lying alone in the ditch as the dirt started to settle around me. It was so quiet you could hear a pin drop, but it soon turned to screams as people started to take stock of the situation. My back was smashed, and blood was squirting from my left ulnar artery as my forearm had been ripped open. A number of dead bodies lay scattered across the ground around me, and I knew if they attacked again I would struggle to defend myself.

Although this had been a traumatic period of my life, when I looked back, my life journey had never been that easy, but at times it also gave me a glimpse into the paranormal world that would give me hope and strength.

I was born into a working class family in Newport, South Wales. A large town about 12 miles east of the welsh capital of Cardiff. My mother Tina worked in retail sales, and my father John was a self-employed car upholsterer who was part of the family's upholstery business. The upholstery business was called Spencers of Newport and was set up by my grandfather in the late 70s. My father and his two brothers made the choice to follow in his trade.

The business premises was a large shop on Corporation Road that was next to Gamberini"'s Fish Bar. My grandparents lived in the flat above, and my mother and father also briefly lived in the flat, and it was there that I was born. We only stayed there for about 11 months before we moved into a 3 bedroom house in Rugby Road, less than half a mile away.

My earliest childhood memory was of time spent in the upholstery shop with my grandfather; I used to earn a small amount of pocket money from them for helping to pick up the rubbish. It was only bits of old cloth and foam, but I was able to use the money to buy lucky bags from the shop down the road.

My grandfather's workshop was at the rear of the building where he would spend his day with his loyal German Shepherd Kim, working on all types of upholstery. The front of the shop served as an upholstery supplies. My grandmother would sell all sorts from sewing materials like sewing cottons and spray adhesives to fabrics and accessories. Occasionally when my mother wasn't working in her retail job she would also help out at the upholstery shop. The family also had a business unit at nearby Jack's pill, and that's where my father and his brothers would operate from. My father specialised in the upholstery of vehicles. A car and coach trimmer, as some might call it.

It was as a toddler that I had my first brush with death. I was spending the afternoon visiting my grandmother and grandfather at the flat. In the flat, there was a large bay window, with a seated area that was shaped to fit the bay window section perfectly.

There were roadwork's being carried out in front of the shop and upon hearing the digger. I had run up to the window jumping up on the seating to take a look, but at the same time I didn't stop. My momentum carried me forward into the glass window. My little body smashed through the old single pane glass, and the only thing that stopped me falling 20 feet to my death was my woollen jumper that my grandmother had nitted got caught on a piece of broken glass. By all accounts, my mother screamed and ran the other way, and it was my father's quick reactions that saved my life.

Most of my early childhood, including my time at nursery, was pretty much like any other with lots of playtime with the other children. That was, at least, until I joined junior school. I was basically a loner in and out of school and very quiet. I'm not sure why, but I just never seemed to fit in with the other kids. I felt like an outcast and was never involved in the other kids' games.

I did have a few friends I would spend time with, but even then, it was like I wasn't there – my opinion was never heard, and I felt invisible. I was also short and skinny, one of the shortest in my year, and with a lack of friends, I soon became a target for bullies.

To begin with, it was only one or two tormentors I had to deal with, but before long, it seemed like everyone wanted to pick on me. I hadn't done anything to them, but they seemed to get pleasure out of making my life a misery. It never really got physical, apart from them pushing me or trying to trip me up. It was more mental threats, stuff to keep me on my toes. "Look out after school", that sort of thing. The bullying would continue daily and it was only on the weekends would I get a break from it.

It was when I was about 9 years old that I had another close incident. This one also involved my family. We had been on a weeks break at Porthmadog in North Wales. My mother at the time was learning to drive, so any opportunity my father would put the L plates on and let her drive. It was a biggish car, an automatic Rover SD1 in blue.

My mother was driving as we headed back to Newport. It was early evening as we were travelling down a country road, the fog came down fast and heavy. Visibility dropped to a few metres. My father told her to pull over so he could take over. As she pulled in, the car behind went past. As my parents were swapping seats, there was a loud smashing noise further up the road. My father quickly drove the 100 or so metres up the road to discover a head-on crash.

The vehicle that had passed us was involved with a elderly couple that, due to the fog, got disorientated and were driving on the wrong side of the road. I remember sitting in the back with my sister when my father went looking for a phone box. There were no mobile phones back in those days, or certainly not as common as today.

As far as I know, there were no fatalities, but the elderly man at the wheel did have a heart attack and was taken to the hospital. As I grew older, I would believe there are no such things as coincidences and that everything happens for a reason, both good and bad.

At home, I also had this crazy thing I had to do before going to bed every night. I couldn't just get into bed and go to sleep. I had a compulsion to do the same thing every night. I would first have to lie on the floor, then I would lie on top of the bed, and finally, I would lie on the bed, but under the sheets. I didn't know why I had to do it, but I did. Not only that. It had to be done to perfection. I was only about 9 years old and thought everyone did stuff like that. Sometimes, it could take me 10 or more attempts and over half an hour until I felt satisfied and could finally get to sleep. It would be many years later before I realised I had OCD.

It was while at junior school that my parents started getting threats over the phone. The house was in bits at the time as my parents had the builders in. My parents kept getting phone calls at all hours from a man claiming to know us and which school we went to. He told them he was planning to kidnap us. Working with BT, the police had to record all phone calls, and for weeks, we had to be taken too and picked up from school by the police. It was the only way to keep us safe. Eventually, the man was found. A middle-aged bloke from the local mental asylum. Apparently he meant us no harm and didn't know us at all. He had just picked a number from the phone book and we became his target.

Back in school, by the time the summer holidays started, I was already beginning to worry about what lay ahead. If I was being bullied in junior school, then what the hell is going to happen in high school. It was a much bigger place, and with kids from lots of other schools there, I was going to get the shit kicked out of me. I remember crying alone in the bathroom a week before starting high school as I knew the bullying was going to continue.

With the new school term starting, I settled in ok during the first week. Even the bullies from my old school left me alone. Maybe they got fed up with it, but who was I kidding. The bullies from my old school just teamed up with those from other schools. I could almost lip read what they were saying... him over there, the short skinny lad...he's soft as shit...he's an easy target, and we bullied him big time in juniors.... He has no friends...Ha-ha...a billy, no mates.

Word must have started to get around that I was a soft touch, easy prey, and before long, I was running a daily gauntlet between classes. Often being kicked and slapped as I made my way down the corridor, some would even grab my school bag and slam it into the ground before throwing it through the window.

The bullies somehow always managed to make sure my packed lunch was destroyed and would rob my dinner money any chance they got. I was constantly on guard, never knowing when or where the next attack was coming from. I couldn't tell the teachers either, as that would just make the situation worse. I couldn't tell my father either because he always told me that if someone picks on you, you hit them once – just once, very hard on the nose. They will get the message.

I could see his point, but my problem was that I was afraid of confrontation and didn't like fighting. Either way, I had to do something, and what I did ultimately affected my education.

I started to become the class clown. I thought if I made people laugh, they would be less likely to pick on me. I was the boy sticking pencils up my nose and throwing rubbers and stuff across the classroom. Looking back now, of course it was a stupid idea, and it wouldn't have made any difference, but back then faced with the bullies every day, I didn't know what else to do.

Over time, my school reports started to deteriorate, and all the teachers had the same thing to say about me; Neil can work hard and produce good results when he wants to, but he is very easily distracted.

This was absolutely true, and I knew I wasn't as stupid or as thick as I came across. However, the bullies were affecting my concentration so much that to everyone, including my own family, I was dumb, immature, and would forever be an embarrassment to them.

There was a small group of lads I hung around with, but like in juniors, I was an outcast, and no one wanted to listen to what I had to say. When it came to team games like football, rugby, or rounders, there was always that one name that was last to be called out, and that was mine.

Maybe it was the fact that I didn't like sport – I was rubbish at all of it. That is, except for one event, and that was running. Only short distance, though. Running the 100 metres, I was a little whippet, most likely from all those years of practice I got legging it from the bullies.

As for a school romance, I could forget it. I was lucky if I got a Christmas card from a girl, let alone a relationship. Needless to say, my confidence suffered a lot. Most of the other boys my age were going out with girls from school, but for me, I hardly got the opportunity to strike up a conversation. It was just another setback.

The bullying continued daily, and leaving school at the end of the day was a nightmare. I had to catch the bus home, which was risky because when the bullies saw me getting on the same bus as them, they'd make sure my journey was full of as much misery as they muster.

Each day, I would hide around the corner watching them line up for the bus from a distance, and only once they had boarded and gone upstairs would I run to get on the bus myself. Even after I was safely on the bus, I would sit near the door for fear that I'd need to make a run for it.

I was shot with a air rifle and on one occasion I was pinned down by a number of individuals while a Clipper lighter was heated up and then pressed deep into the back of my hand. You could smell the burning flesh as the hot wheel worked it's way down to my bone. The individual responsible did eventually get done for ABH.

My grandparents had now retired and moved from Newport to the village of Angle on the South-West Wales coast. They had brought a nice little bungalow on Shirburn close.

During the 6 week summer holidays, I would spend the full duration there with my grandparents and their two German Shepherds, Tara and Kim. No doubt my parents were grateful back home for the peace and quiet they now had.

My grandparents ran a B&B and kept chickens in the garden. Obviously I had fresh eggs for breakfast most mornings. I absolutely loved the place, and it was a break from the school bullies. Angle only had a population of about 200, so everyone knew each other. There was a doctor, a small school, a pub, and a shop that sold the bare minimum, and that was about it. The nearest place for food or other items was in Pembroke, about 10 miles away.

There was just one main road through the village, and from end to end, it was less than a mile. At one end, you had the beach that also had a little lagoon that would fill up on the tide, and at the other end, you had a small harbour. My grandfather had a small rowing boat that he kept in the harbour. Every few days, we would take a trip out in the boat for some proper sea fishing. We also took a small vintage seagull outboard motor just to save on the rowing.

When I was in junior school, my grandfather would often surprise me by being parked outside the school gates on a Friday afternoon in his Commer camper van.

He'd say, "Your mum's packed your clothes, and we are off to Pendine."

My grandparents had a static caravan on the Grove camping site at the top of the hill. Almost every other month, I seemed to be at the caravan and I loved the place.

Many people are familiar with Pendine sands and it's many miles of flat sandy beach that was once home to Malcolm Campbell and all the other land speed records, but just around the corner lay another beach. This one is only about 300 metres in length, and it's called Morfa Bychan, or the secret beach, as I used to think of it.

If you walked to the bottom of the Grove camping site, you would find a rusty old gate onto a very narrow path. This path had dense foliage on each side, but after about a mile, it would lead to the secret beach. It was as a young child that I was on the beach at around 2 a.m., fishing with my uncle when he claimed he saw a UFO moving at speed in various directions high above the water. While I had plenty of great memories at Pendine and Angle, sadly after just 2 years in Angle my grandparents decided to sell up and move back to Newport as my Grandfather had a stroke and his health wasn't so good, and it was far better to be around close family.

My father, at this point, had already been running his own successful car upholstery business for a few years. His business was called Leisuretrim and was based on a farm in Ponthir. Almost every Saturday, I would go to work with him and just help out where I could. He had built himself a great reputation and was probably one of the best car upholsterers in South wales. Well, he was as far as I was concerned.

It was as a 14 year old that I had my first paranormal experience. It was a Sunday, and I had spent all afternoon next door in my neighbours house on the games console. Street fighter we had been playing. Early evening I went back home as I had school next day. I was sitting down on the sofa watching TV while my parents were sitting on the other sofa. Above the TV at head height was an oval mirror with a wooden frame. For some strange reason, I ended fixated on the mirror and in a trance state.

I could clearly see the face of an old man in his early 80s. It was not the face of anyone I knew. From the angle I was sitting, his reflection was coming from the kitchen door that I couldn't see from my sofa due to a partition that separated the living and dining room. After looking away, I took another look, and it was gone. I was so convinced I had seen the person stood by the kitchen door that I got up to take a look. Was it just my imagination or the husband of the previous owner that died many years before. I will never now, but the experience would stay with me for years.

Occasionally, to earn some extra money I would help out at the pill market on a Saturday. My buddy was friends with a man who had a clothing stall, and we would help him in the afternoon to pack the stall away. He used to give us £10 each, which was good money as a kid. One Saturday, as we were close to finishing, we notice a gang of lads watching us from a distance. They wanted our money. As we leave the market, they begin to follow, so we head into the shop. "Put your money in your shoes." Said my mate.

We walk out the shop to be confronted by the gang when one pulls a small knife. "Give us your money."

I said, "We don't have any. We didn't get paid."

We both emptied our pockets in front of them. Thankfully they didn't think to check our shoes and they let us go. Some quick thinking by my mate made the difference that day.

Over the 5 years in high school, living daily with the anxiety caused by these bullies, it really took it out of me. Not just in school time but now at weekends too. I was so anxious about going back when Monday came around that my weekends were ruined as well.

One day I'd had enough of the bullying. It was during a art lesson and I had almost 60 minutes of constant abuse off this individual and could take no more.

Walking out from school I seen the little shit that had been making my life hell, and in one clean motion, I punched him as hard as I could across the face. He dropped to the floor and I quickly disappeared. The following day he turned up looking like he had been hit by Mike Tyson. His face almost looked deformed as it was swollen. I felt a bit guilty and as I had overreacted, but I was soon hit with a conviction for ABH and some compensation to pay out to him.

During my final year in high school, I had the chance for a week of work experience. I had a bit of interest in car mechanics, so I would be spending a week with a local firm. There were about 8 blokes working there with the owner in another unit doing MOTs. On my first day, the lads kept telling me that Friday was my judgement day. I didn't have a clue what they meant, and nobody would tell me.

My days in the garage were spent just keeping the place tidy, fetching tools, and just watching the lads work on the various cars that were coming and going. Just before leaving on the Thursday, they said, "Don't forget tomorrow. It's your judgement day."

Early Friday, one of the lads told me what judgement day was about. They planned to tie my arms behind my back, lift me high on the car ramp, and put hot grease on my balls. Like fuck, I thought. I was a little apprehensive about this judgement day. As the day was coming to an end, I noticed the lads starting to move in on me while forming a circle. I grabbed the nearest thing to me, a large wheel wrench. I shouted out, "Any fucker come close and you're going to get this around your fucking head."

They told me to calm down, and it was only a joke. They weren't going to do anything of the sort. A joke it might have been to them, after many years of constant bullying, I'd had enough of it. I told them that I couldn't promise that I wouldn't have used the wrench on them. A couple of weeks later, I was asked if I wanted to go back to the garage for another week. I did, and this time, there was no judgement day. I worked well with the lads all week, and come Friday, the owner gave me a pay packet.

By the time I came to sit my GCSE exams, it was too late, I had blown any chance of getting decent grades, and I didn't really care. I took nothing positive from school, and I couldn't wait to just get it all over with. My grades ended up as I expected. Terrible. This wasn't a shock for my parents, as they weren't expecting anything more from me.

When I went to the job centre, reality soon hit. Every job I looked at seemed to be out of my league. My only real option was an agency. I signed up with a company called Kelter Recruitment that was based in town. They didn't have any positions for me, but they did offer me a place on their 6-week in-house course that would earn me an NVQ Level 1 in electronics. This would open up a few positions they did have.

The pay was a mere £45 a week and could hardly be considered a wage, but it was better than nothing. After my training I was told they would find me full time work where I could utilise my new skill. The course was easy and covered mostly printed circuit board (PCB) assembly and soldering. As soon as the course was over, as promised, I was offered a job at a Panasonic warehouse. The job was alright and paid a reasonable wage, but it didn't last, and I soon found myself unemployed.

Over the next 12 months, I ended up in a variety of different jobs, all of which offered little financial security or job satisfaction. I even worked as a security guard at one point. Back then, before the days of SIA rules, anyone could do the job even if you had a string of criminal convictions. I later started working security for the budget supermarket Kwik Save. It was based 11 miles away in Pontypool, and because I couldn't drive, my father would drop me off, and in the evening, I would find my own way home.

One Friday evening I planned to hit the nightclubs after work but the bus wasn't running and I didn't have money for a taxi. To make things worse, with my shirt, trousers, and shoes, I was hardly kitted out for a jog home. I turned it into a fast walk, and two and half hours later, I finally made it home. A further 45 minutes later and I was showered, dressed, and in town, sipping a chilled pint of Guinness. That was my first taste of a long-distance walk.

Another job became available at a furniture manufacturing factory in Rogerstone, and because my uncle worked there as their head of design, I was given the job. It was a good place to work, I started at 08:00 and finished at 16:30. My days were spent making the fabric faces that go on the front of sofas, along with other upholstery production line stuff.

I was also in the process of learning to drive and things were starting to look up After a few months of lessons, I passed my test and took out a bank loan for £1,000 to purchase my very own car. I wanted something quick and sporty. My father used to own a Mk3 Ford Escort XR3I in rosso red, which I loved, and I really wanted one for myself. But being 18 years old and inexperienced, there was no way I could afford to insure one. I had to look for something else.

I came across a 1998 Nissan sunny coupe in black. It looked a little bit like the Knight Rider car, and the owner only wanted a grand for it, so I bit his hand off at the chance. As soon as I brought it home, I set about trying to tart it up a bit. Chrome racing pedals, a loud exhaust tail pipe, and a Kenwood CD player just for starters.

One day I had my best buddy in the car with me, and I was driving a little too fast. Meatloaf's Hit song, Bat out of hell was playing when the blue flashing light came up behind. I pulled over, and the officer came up to my window. He shouted, "What the heck do you think you're doing flying down this road like a bat out of hell." I looked at my buddy and giggled. I said, "Sorry, officer, it's just because we were listening to bat out of hell."

The officer sadly didn't find it as funny as I did and gifted me with a 7 day producer. Over a number of months I must of visited the police station at least have a dozen times due to my driving habits. My parents thought I was such a sensible driver, but little did they realise just how reckless I was becoming.

In the back of my mind, I wanted to prove my worth. I was fed up of the constant criticism I was receiving, and in many ways it was justified. So I decided it was time to grow up and make myself and my family proud.

Chapter 2

Para's insight course.

I WAS STILL working at the upholstery factory at the time, but not for much longer. One day, when I got home from work, I told my parents that I was planning to join the army and that I was going into the careers office in the morning for more information.

"What are you thinking of joining?" My father asked.

"The Parachute Regiment", I said.

My father thought I was mad. He did have a point. I was scared of heights for a start, and as for my fitness, well, I wasn't even sure.

I went out for a short run just to find out, and after less than a mile, I had to turn back as I couldn't breathe. Years of heavy smoking had finally caught up with me. If I was going to prove my worth to the doubters, something major had to happen.

To start off with I quit the fags, and then joined a gym. The gym was only a 5-minute walk away so it was ideal. I began training straight away but was slow to start. Fifteen to twenty minutes on the treadmill and I was knackered.

Day after day, I would spend just 20 minutes on the treadmill. I never seemed to be able to last any longer. Then, one day, I turned up, and there was a notice of the machine. It read that anyone who completes 30 minutes on this machine can get a free fitness gift. I thought I'd give it a go. As per usual, at the 20-minute point, I was just about to hit the stop button when I had the thought, just 10 more minutes. I reached the 30-minute point and felt great. My breathing had regulated, and I was into a nice, comfortable rhythm. I ended up staying on for an hour. That was it. There were no more 20 minute runs. I started training twice a day.

In the morning I'd hit the weights hard, and then I would do 2 hours of cardio in the evening. My daily routine was: 1 hour on the treadmill covering around 14km, followed by 30 minutes on the stationary bike and 30 minutes on the rowing machine. I was becoming fit and could run 5 miles in just 30 minutes. I also began to try a bit of speed marching. I had a cheap rucksack that I stuffed with pillows for padding and 15kg in dumbbells to add weight.

I used to walk as fast as I could from my house to the 14 Locks Canal Centre. It was a few miles each way, taking me just under 2 hours to finish. The minute I felt fit enough, I went to the careers office.

As I walked through the door, a recruiting sergeant approached me.

The sergeant said, "How can I help you?"

"I want to join the Para's." I replied.

Like most jobs, staff have targets to meet, and army recruitment is no different. They want you to join their Regiment because it looks good for them and also keeps the numbers up in the Regiment. They will always try their best to convince you.

He said, "How about joining a Welsh infantry Regiment?"

"No thanks," I said, "I've made up my mind".

After about 10 minutes of him showing me some video clips of the Welsh Regiments, he gave in.

"Ok Neil, the parachute Regiment. A weekend insight course at their Aldershot Barracks will give you a taste of the Regiment and also a chance to see how you stand up in terms of fitness. I will book you in on the next available course, and once you get there, work hard and give it your all".

I had a few weeks to wait before the course began, so I made sure I sustained my fitness to stay in tip top condition. The day I arrived at Aldershot station, I met up with a load of other lads from all over the country who were also joining me on the course.

WE WERE CHATTING about what they might have planned for us when a number of Land Rovers turned up. They were there to take us to Browning barracks. The home of the Parachute Regiment. Once we got to the barracks we were taken to the accommodation block and issued with a bed space and some itchy brown blankets. Looking at the bed, I wasn't sure if the floor was more comfortable. We were then ushered into a lecture room for a briefing with the training Company Sergeant Major and some of his staff. The CSM gave us a quick introduction of himself and his staff, the weekend's itinerary, and what was required of us. Which, as the Para's put it, was: plenty of grit, guts, and gumption.

After the briefing, we had a chance to chill out in the NAAFI and talk to some of the serving lads. One piece of advice they bestowed upon us was to stick to the "2-pint rule" as there was plenty of physical work coming up in the morning. It's fair to say that not everyone including myself stuck to it.

At 05:30 the following morning, the training staff came in to wake us up.

He shouted out, "Right you lot, get your bed space squared away, get dressed in your PT kit and be outside in fifteen minutes."

We lined up in two ranks and walked smartly to the canteen for breakfast. We were not yet in the military, so there was no marching requirement, but they still made sure we looked smart as we moved around the barracks. The choice of food was awesome, you had the healthy option like fruit, cereal and toast – or like me you could go for the greasy fry-up.

Half an hour after eating, we had to get ready for our first test of the day. The Basic Fitness Test ("BFT").

The BFT consisted of three tests against the clock; press ups and sit-ups with the maximum number of reps you could manage in 2 minutes, followed by a timed run over 3 miles. I can't remember what I scored on the first two tests, but I know I passed. As we lined up outside for the run, the Regiment's PTI came out carrying two black bags. He tipped them out, and a load of old and worn combat boots fell out.

He shouted, "Right then, just find yourself a pair that fit and get lined up behind me".

Rummaging through the pile, I found a pair of size 9's and chucked them on. Looking around at the other guys, I could see all shapes and sizes. Some were wiry fit looking men, and some looked like they could move mountains. As far as the military is concerned, size doesn't matter. Only the will to win.

The PTI set the pace, and we had 15 minutes to cover the first mile and half. It was easy, and I barely broke a sweat, though some of the boys were already falling behind. The halfway point was at queen's parade, a large grassy area in the middle of Aldershot military town.

We had a 30-second rest before the return leg.

"Right," said the PTI, "this is now individual best effort and you're looking for nine and a half minutes' tops, don't be the last man home.... Standby.... GO".

I sprinted off, but the boots slowed me down more than if I had been wearing my trusty old trainers. There were about six lads in front of me, and they were really flying along. I had the PTI on my heels telling me to catch up to them, but I couldn't, I was exhausted. I reached the final straight and saw that the fastest runners were already home. The first man finished in less than 7 minutes, a staggering time in trainers, but in boots, it was even more impressive. I crossed the line breathless in 9 minutes 4 seconds, not brilliant but still well within the cut-off time, while some were still coming in after 12 minutes.

After the physical tests, we had a shower before being given a tour of the museum and an introduction to P Company. P company, or Pre Parachute selection course, was a number of tests that have to be passed before you are accepted onto parachute training and can serve with the airborne forces. It's known as the toughest British Army selection course outside of the Special Forces. There's a log run, stretcher carry, milling, high-level confidence course, plus two, ten, and twenty-mile endurance marches to complete. The events are run over a week, and if you score enough points, you pass. That evening, we enjoyed some more down time in the NAAFI with only the beep test to complete in the morning.

We had a final chat with the CSM about our performance over the weekend and the next steps from there before we were given a packed lunch and dropped back at the station.

Sadly, or more stupidly, after only a few days being back home, it all went wrong. I ended up crashing my car into a roundabout at speed. My car was wedged into a barrier, and no matter how hard I tried, it wouldn't move. My mate gave me a lift home to collect my toolbox so I could remove the bumper and free my car. When I returned to the crash scene, the police had already turned up, and eyewitnesses had come forward to give statements about my driving. It was my first experience in police custody. Just those 4 walls and a solid steel door to look at. It gives you plenty of time to reflect on what's happened.

I was now charged with four driving offences.
Dangerous driving.
Motor racing on a public highway.

Hit and run.
Failing to report an accident.

This was madness. Apparently, it was a hit and run because I hit the barrier and left the scene without leaving my details. Err ok, I thought. As for failing to report the accident. I felt sure I had 24 hours to notify them, and they had spoken to me at the scene of the accident only an hour later. The other two offences I couldn't argue with. With statements now taken, I was awaiting a court appearance. When I got home my father went absolutely bonkers with me. The car was a definite insurance write-off.

When I went back to the careers office and told them what happened, they said, "Your report from Aldershot was good, but unfortunately, you can't continue your application until the case is settled". No way. I was gutted, but I couldn't blame anyone. It was my own stupid fault. I had no choice but to wait for the court outcome, but time and time again, it was adjourned. This happened six times before a final verdict was eventually given. Standing nervously in Newport Magistrates as my fate was delivered.

I WAS CLEARED of all but one – dangerous driving. My punishment was a 12-month ban with an extended retest and a fine of £825, which in today's rate is about £1500. Although I wouldn't know it at the time, the driving ban would be the best thing that could of happened. It gave me chance to grow up. While on the surface I was old enough to drive, in reality I just wasn't mature enough. I was a boy racer. I can't even begin to explain just how crazy I was behind the wheel. I was just so lucky I hadn't killed myself or someone else.

I went back into the careers office to inform them of the outcome, and this time, I was told I couldn't continue until my fine had been paid off. Bloody hell, was this ever going to happen. With the wages I was earning, it would take ages. I only had to pay a repayment plan of £15 a week, but I needed to pay a lot more if I was ever going to get signed up.

After several months of paying off the fine, my father generously paid off the last of what I owed. Maybe he was fed up with my troublemaking and wanted me out of the house too.

This time, when I went back to the careers office, I was feeling confident, but once again, I was hit with another setback. Op Barras, the daring rescue that saw men from 1 Para and 22 SAS attack the west side boys, the brutal militia group who were holding a number of members from the Royal Irish Regiment hostage. Except for the loss of one man, the operation was a success and raised publicity for recruitment for the Para's.

For me, though, it was bad news, as my recruiter told me I now had several months on the waiting list for the Para's, or I could go with my second choice. As part of the recruitment process, you choose three different units in the event of shortage or other reasons. My first choice was obviously Para reg, my second was the Royal Welch Fusiliers ("RWF"), and my third was the military police.

Now, with a long wait for the Para's, I was met with the choice of joining the Fusiliers, which had a shorter waiting time. It wasn't an ideal situation, but I could hardly go back home without some positive news, and anyway, I thought, when I pass out of training, I can just request a transfer. Well was the plan. Before I could begin training, I still had tests to complete. One was called the British Army Recruitment Battery ("BARB"), a simple touch screen test that considers your school grades and determines what role you'd be most suitable for. It was an easy test with questions such as, "If this cog turns this way, which way does this one turn?", not exactly rocket science.

Another thing I had to pass was the recruit selection centre, which was run at Pirbright and covered an assortment of tests, including a medical and some physical trials. I ended up being sent home within an hour of turning up. I failed the medical. It seems I forgot to mention that I had asthma as a child and now required a doctor's note before I could continue. The second time, everything went well, and I passed all of the tests with flying colours. All that was left to do now was the Oath of Allegiance. I signed the oath at the careers office in front of a military officer and thought, this is it, my future is now sealed.

Chapter 3

Lichfield.

MY TRAINING WAS due to start in just 2 weeks, and while I couldn't wait to get started, I was also a little apprehensive. The training was going to last for 26 weeks in total, provided I didn't pick up an injury or get back-squadded.

The first 12 weeks is Basic Training or the common military syllabus as it's generally called, and would take place in Lichfield, in Staffordshire. The idea of basic training was all about taking you from your civilian life and getting you to the level of skill and discipline a trained soldier has, and ready to learn your new trade.

After you complete your basic training you move on to phase 2 – trade training. It doesn't matter what role in the military you are training for; be it infantry, engineering, military police or even a chef, everyone has the same 12 weeks of basic training with only the trade training being different in length.

My trade training was to take place at the infantry training centre in Catterick, a military town stuffed away in the north Yorkshire moors. These intense 14 weeks were known as the Combat Infantryman's Course and produced some of the best and most inspired infantrymen the world over. These days new infantry recruits complete both their basic and phase 2 at Catterick, but back in 2002, basic was held in Lichfield.

The day arrived for my training to begin, and I boarded the train from Newport to Lichfield with my suitcase packed full of new clothes and a kit list of items I needed to take with me. Of course, Kiwi black shoe polish was a must. As the train pulled into Lichfield station, I could see that the place was full of lads from all over the country. We were all ready to begin a new journey of life.

A coach soon turned up with a few members of the training staff.

A corporal shouted out, "One straight line facing me.

When I call your name out, you reply with 'Yes Corporal'.

"Spencer?"

"Yes, corporal." I shouted out.

Apart from one person everyone else was accounted for. "Right, grab your bags and get yourselves on the coach." Said a member of the training staff.

This was it. There was no going back now.

Once we arrived at Whittington Barracks we were escorted to our rooms and given an hour to settle into our new environment. Including myself, there were eight of us in the room. We were complete strangers at that moment, but you could be sure that by the end of our training we would know each other better than we knew ourselves or our own families.

We were chatting amongst ourselves when a member of the training staff came into the room.

"Alright lads, my name is Corporal Smith, I will be your section commander for the duration of your time here at Lichfield. When you speak to me, you will address me as 'Corporal'. I'm here to make sure you get through this course, so if you have any problems, please don't hesitate to ask."

The initial week was going to be pretty straightforward with a bit of paperwork to fill out and another medical exam to go through. With the administration out of the way it was time for us to visit the stores and issued with our new kit, and there was a lot of it.

4 pairs of socks
2 pairs of trousers
2 shirts

2 jackets
1 Gore-Tex jacket and matching trousers
2 pairs of boots
A helmet
One S10 respirator

And all of our gym kit which consisted of a pair of shorts, a t-shirt, and a fancy pair of trainers called Silver Shadows. This was all crammed into a large black holdall. Oh, I almost forgot. We were also given our regimental beret, although we wouldn't be allowed to wear it until after week 6, that's providing we passed off the square.

It weighed us down as we struggled to carry our stuff back to our rooms. This lot of gear was only part of our issued kit. After lunch, we would be issued with our loadcarrying equipment and everything else we would need when out on the ground. We all formed a large circle as the quartermaster passed out more kit.

120 litre Bergen
Webbing pouches and straps
Mess tins
A digging tool
A large sleeping bag with Gore-Tex liner
Plus, a single foam roll mat

Later that day, Corporal Smith asked us to go to his room as he wanted to teach us some skills. Sadly, it wasn't shooting skills we would be learning that day but those of another deadly weapon… the steam iron.

He spent about 2 hours demonstrating how we were expected to iron each piece of clothing, with only intentional creases permitted. The creases of sleeves and the front pleats of trousers had to be so sharp they looked like they could draw blood. These creases were the result of high heat, plenty of steam, and a spray of starch, combined with some good old elbow grease. He then showed us how to fold t-shirts using a piece of A4 paper and also how to fold our socks. They would be folded up in such a way that it would create a face. We were told that for the first 4 weeks, the socks would present with a sad face, and for the weeks 4 to 8 they would have a relaxed look, and weeks 8 to the end of basic, you guessed it, a happy face. After he'd finished with the clothing. We were shown how to assemble our webbing and pouches. We had pouches for our magazines, not the type you read, but those for holding ammunition. There was a large pouch for holding mess tins and food. We had one for our water bottle and also another for our digging tool. The Webbing had to fit comfortably. Any lose straps would have to be taped up and there couldn't be any rattling when moving around.

We were also shown how to shape our berets. This was done by alternating between hot and cold water and then letting it dry. Like a idiot I had left mine on my head overnight to dry, and the following morning, my pillow was blue as the dye had run.

We were sent back to our rooms and found a laminated piece of A4 paper on our beds, revealing a detailed locker arrangement. By the following morning, we were all expected to have our kit set out exactly as it was shown on the layout. The hangers all had to be matching. Wooden if possible. They had to be a set distance apart. Something like 2 fingers. Trousers folded and hanging to the correct length. The shirts and jackets would have to face the same way with the razor sharp, well pressed sleeves on display.

Beneath would be folded T-shirts that would look as smart as in any top end designer shop. You would also have a soap placed neatly on top of the dish. Toothbrush and paste would also have to be at the required distance apart. At the bottom would be a highly polished pair of military boots that would be stood to attention. Most of us were up well past midnight, making sure we had completed the task properly and everything looked immaculate and identical to Corporal Smith's detail.

After only a few hours' sleep it was time to get up and get ready for the 05:30 locker inspection.

We were dressed smartly in our well pressed, brand new military uniforms when we heard the order, "Stand by your beds!"

As corporal Smith approached the bed, we had to slam our left foot hard into the floor whilst shouting out our name, rank, and number. Corporal Smith would then start inspecting our bed space and locker like a crime scene investigator. It seemed that no matter how much time and effort was put in, you could be sure that the training staff would find something that wasn't quite up to standard. The punishment would come in the form of a show parade. It would normally take place around 8 or 9 pm, thus taking away your evening time. You would be required to turn up in whatever uniform they asked and to be immaculate. I would end up spending more than my fair share of time at these evening parades during basic.

Later on in the day came what I was dreading the most. The Haircut. I was young looking anyway and struggled to buy cigarettes without ID, so I knew it was going to be dramatic, and it was. With a number 1 all over, I looked about 12 years old and ready to join the cadets and not the big boys Army.

I was starting to make some good friends and had become friends with a couple of guys, Dave Harris and Lagi. Dave was joining the Welsh Fusiliers. Lagi was a Fijian and was a mountain of a man. Well over 6 foot, solid and full of muscle. He wouldn't have looked out of place standing next to Jonah Lomu. Lagi was not the sort of person you'd want to upset. He was one of the quietest and also one of the strongest blokes I'd ever met. Only once did I ever see him lose his temper when some idiot was spoiling for a fight. Picking on Lagi was not the brightest idea this lad had come up with, and it took a large number of men to restrain Lagi and stop him from tearing the antagonising little shit apart.

During the next few weeks we were taught the basics of marching with hours spent going up and down the parade square until our ankles were burning. For some of the boys it took a little time to get used to it as they lacked the prerequisite co-ordination. This was evident in the way they would move both left arm and left leg at the same time, also known as "tick tocking".

There were also many hours in the classroom learning about military history, the military rank structure, map reading, and basic first aid. In our second week, we were introduced to our personal weapon: the SA80 assault rifle. There was a lot of class work to cover before we would get the chance to unleash on the firing range, and that wouldn't be until week 5.

During lessons we were taught all the working principles of the weapon, how to fully strip, assemble and clean the weapon, before moving on to the handling drills of how to load and unload safely, as well as how to deal with stoppages and other troubleshooting advice. Weapon safety was paramount, and only once the instructors believed we had acquired the necessary skill and respect owed to the weapon would we be allowed to use live rounds on the range.

Towards the end of week 2, we got our first taste of living in the field during "Exercise First Night" where you spend just one night out in the field. It would give us a taste of what was to come as there were plenty of nights in the field ahead of us.

Living in the field is an important aspect of training and one that can take a lot of people by surprise. We had to learn how to pack a Bergen properly which is a skill in itself. As a kid on a day trip for example you would most likely throw all of your kit into a rucksack in any old order and it would suffice. But that's not how things work in the military. A Bergen contains the complete kit required to survive while out on the ground. Not only must our kit be kept in a clean and serviceable condition, We were told there was a place for everything, and everything must be in its place.

We should never have to search for stuff in our Bergen. We should know where everything is at any time. When operating at night, there would be times when light couldn't be used. The last thing you wanted to be doing was pulling everything out of the bergen, only to discover later that you have left items behind. A fully packed Bergen can weigh upwards of 100lbs, so it needs to be prepared correctly and in good order. Ideally, things like spare clothes, your sleeping bag, and things you use the least would all go at the bottom of the bag, with the things you need most towards the top.

All clothing items would also need to be placed in sealed bags to keep them dry in case of a heavy downpour or river crossing. Items like GoreTex and warm kit can go in the top flap or side pouches for quick access, along with your food and water.

While out in the field, we were taught how to set up camp, how to build a shelter, and basic patrol formations amongst other things. Some things would just get easier with experience. After my first night patrol, it was very cold and I made the mistake of wearing all my warm kit in my sleeping bag. I was lovely and warm while I was in it, until morning came I was a sweating mess. Then I just got cold as I didn't have any warm kit to put on. Afterwards I would sleep with just my T shirt and trousers on, and place all my warm kit at the bottom of my sleeping bag. My body heat would keep it warm for the morning.

It was all a learning curve and really exciting stuff, apart from night sentry and the morning routine. Being woken up at 02:00 to sit in what could be a water filled ditch for 2 hours was not the most pleasant of experiences but it was all an essential part of military life that everyone had to experience. When on night sentry, it was far better to be the first or last man to take turn. At least you wouldn't get any broken sleep. I really disliked the morning routine as there was so much to get done in a short period of time. There was weapon cleaning, a hot meal to cook, you had to have a wash, powder your feet and be ready for an inspection within about an hour.

Week 5 approached, and it was almost time for us to visit the live firing range, but first, we had to pass the weapon handling test. One by one, we were called into a room where the instructor would throw a load of commands at us, all of which had to be demonstrated without fault. Everything was covered in the test from loading to unloading, to making safe and stoppage drills. Some people needed a second chance but everyone got there in the end.

We were soon out on the firing range hitting targets out to 400 metres using various positions. We started off in prone, which is lying down. This is by far the best and most accurate position, while also making yourself the smallest target for the enemy. We then moved on to squatting, kneeling, and standing. We would also be required to hit targets while wearing our respirator.

To begin with, we would have to zero our rifles. This was used to align the sights to the rifle. We would fire one round at a time and make small adjustments on the sight until all rounds were tightly grouped together. Once the rifles were zeroed, hitting targets out to 100m was little more than point and shoot, but beyond that range the fall of the round and the wind direction had to be taken into consideration and adjusted accordingly. We put into practice all the marksmanship principles that we had been taught in the previous weeks. Things like making sure the weapon points naturally at the target. How to control your breathing and how we shouldn't snatch the trigger, but to just take up the slack and gradually pull. Thus, to avoid any sudden jerking.

Throughout our training we would spend a fair bit of time on the range regardless of the weather conditions. It could be a long day, but there was one part of the day that we all looked forward too. Lunchtime. When you saw the 4 ton trucks in the far distance, you knew food was coming. The catering team would set up like a production line and bring out these large food containers that would be full of hot stew. We'd line up with our tins and receive two large scoops and two pieces of bread. There would also be some hot tea and coffee. After hours on the range in wet and cold conditions, this would definitely raise a smile.

One part of training that a few of us were dreading was the gas chamber. We had practised a fair bit in our NBC drills. Kitted out in our full NBC clothing (nuclear, biological, and chemical) and our S10 respirator. Around 10 of us made our way into the chamber.

A member of training staff let off a number of tear gas canisters and the room soon filled up. We had to trust our respirators so the staff made us carry out a number of movements. From canister changers to jogging on the spot. Sooner or later the worst bit was upon us.

We were called forward one at a time to the training staff.

He said, "I want you to remove your mask and say your name, rank, and number."

I got as far as my rank, and then the tear gas hit. It was the most horrible experience I'd faced. I couldn't breathe, and my eyes were burning. The training staff grabbed me and pushed me out the door.

"Face the wind, and don't touch your eyes." Shouted a member of the training staff. It was tempting to rub the eyes, but that would just make it worse, as we would just be rubbing it deeper into the eyes. The wind would soon blow the stuff out.

With another few nights on exercise out the way, week 6 was upon us. We were now halfway through basic. It was at this point that we would be allowed home for a long weekend, but there were some things we had to do first. There would be a full inspection. This would be not only your personal bedspace and locker but the full accommodation block. The Company sergeant major and company commander would be present for this. We would then move outside to pass off the square. We would be required to march alone smartly and correctly and also answer a number of questions about the regiment's history that we would eventually be a member of.

We had a marching test to pass first, and a few questions on the history of the regiment you were joining. If we passed both of them then we'd earn a long weekend at home. Even better, upon our return we could replace our baseball caps for regimental berets. In my historical test I was asked when the Royal Welch Fusiliers were formed and by whom.

"1689 sir, by Lord Herbert of Chirbury, Sir."

"Correct."

That was it, I had gotten myself a weekend pass in my own bed! Everyone was pleased. We had only known each other for 6 weeks, but we were living in each other's' pockets 24/7 and had become a brotherhood. It would be a shame to see someone have to stay the weekend when most people were back home. Everyone deserved the break. Not that I believed they would hold anyone back.

When I arrived at Newport station I was surprised to see my father waiting there for me. It wasn't like him so I knew something was wrong. He didn't have good news. He said "While you've been away your mother was diagnosed with breast cancer. She's waiting for a date to begin treatment"

When I saw her I thought the best thing to do was to be positive, but instead she was the more positive one by acting totally normal and asking how my training was going. I tried not to mention the cancer and just told her how I was getting along.

Most of the weekend was spent in the pub with nights out in a club or two, just making the most of my freedom. The weekend flew by and it was soon time to return to Lichfield. I gave my mother a kiss and wished her well with her upcoming chemotherapy.

The next 6 weeks were more or less the same as before but with more time spent in the field building up on our field craft skills. The staff would use what they called the red light game to test our camouflage and patrolling skills in the dark. In the far distance, there would be a red light. This would normally be the rear light of a vehicle. It was our mission to get to the red light without being caught by members of the training team, who had various bits of equipment like night vision at their disposal.

We were told there would be some privileges for those who make it. As soon as the flare was let off, it was our signal to go. Surprisingly, only myself and another lad made it to the light without getting caught. We were treated to hot bacon rolls and coffee, but most importantly, a night off evening sentry.

As the last few weeks were coming to an end, we had a few tests to complete. One of those was our shooting test on the range. We were expected to hit a number of targets, using various firing positions and at different distances. On my test, I failed. I would get another chance the next day, but if I failed again, there was a possibility that I could end up being back squadded. This I wasn't too keen on as it meant going over the same weeks again. Thankfully, I passed the shoot the next day. We also had another BFT to see how we fared after almost 3 months of constant gym sessions and forced speed marches.

As soon as we picked up our No.2 parade uniform, we knew we were inching closer to the passing out parade. When week 12 arrived, our final week, it turned out to be what felt like the longest week in history. There were loads of last-ditch preparations to make sure everything would go to plan. There would also be a final locker inspection to white glove standard. Like many others, I chose to sleep on the floor in my sleeping bag that night, so I didn't need to iron the bed sheets early in the morning.

My mother had now been having regular chemotherapy sessions, and her treatment was coming along fine. Both my parents travelled up for my passing out parade, and it was definitely a proud moment.

I now had the joy of a two week break at home before I would move onto Catterick, and start the Combat infantryman's course.

From what I had been told Catterick would be more relaxed, and it was true to a certain extent. It would be much more on the physical side. There would still be locker inspections and so on, but as we had passed phase 1, we were now classed as trained soldiers and were therefore expected to maintain a sense of discipline without the need for constant checks.

Chapter 4

Catterick.

THIS WAS IT. We now had 14 tough weeks ahead on our Combat Infantryman's course. As we arrived at Vimy barracks, we were greeted by a sign outside bearing a shield and bayonet with the words, "School of Infantry", written underneath.

This is where shit gets real.

While our basic training in Lichfield was turning us from a civilian to a soldier. The combat infantryman's course was about taking us from a basic soldier to one of the best fighting combat soldiers on the planet.

This stage was going to be much more physically demanding than basic, but it also came with some benefits. Those benefits came in the form of luxury items. We were allowed to use our own bedding, and could have things like music systems, TV's, and PlayStations, but put one foot wrong and you would soon be back to itchy blankets and whatever music you had on your phone. To most people they sound like insignificant items, but to us it was positively indulgent compared to what we were used to.

The training staff came to welcome us and I was placed under section commander Corporal Gareth Redfern. He was also a member of the Fusiliers and had gone to the same school as me, although he was a few years older. Gareth had joined the Fusiliers straight from school and had a good number of years' experience behind him. There was no doubt he had the skills and knowledge to get us into shape.

We also met our new platoon sergeant. Sergeant John D Williams who was also a member of the Fusiliers. He had plenty of years of operational experience behind him, and he was someone I would become good friends with many years later.

There would be plenty of speed marching throughout our time at Catterick, and the training area was perfect for it. By the end of our training, we would have to pass the ICFT otherwise known as The Infantry Combat Fitness Test. The CFT was an 8-mile speed march carrying 44lbs of kit and a rifle. That's a total of 55lb and with just 2 hours to do it. This would be done on the training area. The training area was mostly gravel tracks with rolling hills.

Another fitness test on the training area was the 2 miler. Carrying 25kg including your webbing, helmet, and rifle. We would tab out 2 miles as a group in 30 minutes, and then it was 2 miles individual best effort back with a strict cut-off time of 18 minutes.

I loved speed marching and found that I had a natural ability to move fast as hell while carrying the weight of a small child on your back. I'm sure all the training I did alone while preparing for the Parachute Regiment was what helped build up my physical and mental endurance. In addition to speed marching, there was also a multitude of other physical tests to get through, such as the Beep Test, assault course, steeplechase, gym sessions, and ever-present BFT.

Two weeks into training we had the bayonet range to face, and what a day that was. From first thing in the morning we were run ragged and constantly made to feel stressed out and angry. It was aimed at gradually building up our aggression so that when it was time to face the dummies we would go all out like men possessed. It was a long day but I fully enjoyed it, although I cant say I would feel the same doing it in a real situation.

The daily locker inspections continued, albeit at a much more laid back pace. If we did mess up, there was a punishment they liked to dish out that was a dress parade. You were given a number of minutes to get changed into whichever kit the training staff chose to call out. This could mean going through every item in your wardrobe which you had just spent the entire evening ironing to precision. A popular and quite a funny one was the turtle. Wearing black combat boots, green long johns and t-shirt, you would tuck your green sleeping bag into your waist, under your legs and over your back. With the helmet on you can just picture the scene.

We were allowed most weekends off but as it was too far to travel back to South Wales every weekend, some of the lads and I made use of the bars in town. There was one main hot spot we liked to frequent which was a club that just so happened to be the place every other service person went too, and for good reason. The place was a shithole and your feet would stick to the floor if you stood still for more than a few seconds, but on the upside you paid a small entry fee and all drinks were free. For a young squaddie this was great, but also a recipe for disaster as Regiment rivalry and fights were extremely common.

One Saturday evening our night almost ended before it had even begun. It was a couple of miles walk into town and wasn't uncommon for one of us to need a piss along the way. Sprawling woodland lined our left as we walked down Scotton road. Normally, we would step over the dividing wall, which was only about a foot high, walk in a few feet, and do our business.

On this particular evening, one of the lads, a short lad called Richie, said he needed a piss. He ran ahead of us and hopped over the low wall. After a few minutes he still hadn't returned, even as we started shouting out for him, there was no reply. What the hell is he playing at? A bit puzzled, I went to take a look. The area in which he had jumped over was in fact a bridge with a drop into a stream. He was lying there motionless, face down in the dark water.

We called out to him but got no reply, and he still didn't move. Myself and another lad climbed down to get to him. We attempted to wake him again but still no joy. We knew we had to get him back up somehow, so decided we would lift from the bottom while others at the top would pull him up towards them. Looking down from the top it was an incredibly steep and slippery bank, and although he only weighed about 10 stone, trying to lift an unconscious man proved no easy task. While we were hauling him up, another lad was on the road trying to flag down a vehicle whilst he called for an ambulance on his phone.

We managed to get him up and thankfully he came around. The knock on the head must have been a good one to take him out for so long. We propped him up against the wall and draped a jacket over his body to keep him warm while we waited for the military police to turn up. The police took a few statements and left it at that because fortunately it was just an accident. The lad made a full recovery and was back in training the next day. Sadly, I found out years later that he had died in a motorcycle accident back home.

Another incident we had following a night out in the club involved a group of Fijian lads. The lads were short and stocky. Strong as a ox. They were good guys and good soldiers, but they seemed to struggle with drink. After a meagre 2 pints they wanted to fight the world and we became an easy target for drunken louts looking for trouble. During these alcohol-fuelled brawls, having Jo with us was a blessing. Built like a heavyweight boxer with a punch to match, I'd never seen a man take out so many so fast. It was like a scene from the film Hooper with bodies being flung across tables.

That evening, after getting back from the club, I was woken up to find one of the Fijian lads at the foot of my bed.

"Were you in the club tonight?" he asked.

"Yeah, why?" I replied.

Crack. The punch hit me right in the face.

He said, "I will ask you again…. Were you in the club tonight?"

Once again, I replied, "Yes…"

I'm punched in the face again. I could feel the blood now dripping from my nose. The punches didn't hurt, probably because I was still drunk.

He ordered me to wait there while he left the room. Most likely to get more of his mates to batter me. Like fuck, I thought. As soon as he left the room I got dressed and legged it round to Jo's room.

Banging like hell on his door, as soon as he saw my face he flipped, pulling out his entrenching tool he began to screw it together.

"Bloody hell mate," I said, "it's not that serious, I don't want you to kill the bastard."

Thankfully, he put it away, the last thing you need at the start of your military career is an assault charge on your record. A report was logged about what happened and we never had any more problems after that.

By this time, our training had intensified, and the field exercises were getting longer and longer. We also had an introduction to setting up defensive positions. We would spend hours digging a trench, only to be told to grab our kit and prepare to move. We would then tab a few kilometres and start again from scratch. Again, we would be told to move. By the third time we were all getting pissed off. The trenches were almost dug when from the distance I could see a JCB digger. It was coming to finish the job for us. The idea was to teach us that war isn't predictable and that just digging your trench doesn't mean soon getting your head down. The battle picture can change at any time.

Once our defensive positions were sorted, we could start getting into our daily routine. Alternating between time on sentry, cleaning weapons, eating, or just getting some sleep. Before joining the military, I'd never been one to sleep during the day, regardless of how little I'd had the night before. I'd normally just stay awake until night-time, but this place was different. We were constantly on the move, and you never knew when the next time for a kip would come, so any opportunity you got, you'd get your head down.

While in the field, we would continue to practise our contact and patrolling skills. It was all coming together and I felt at home doing something I enjoyed and felt I was good at. Our final exercise was a big-un: a 2-week battle camp running through everything we had been taught throughout our 14-week infantry course. This would culminate with a full live firing contact scenario with hundreds of us together working towards a common goal.

The exercise was conducted in Otterburn, close to the Scottish border. The place was bloody freezing, and I couldn't wait to just be done with it all. It was an exhausting and challenging experience but thoroughly enjoyed all round.

With the final exercise completed, we were now free to relax a little and look forward to our passing out parade. My mother's cancer treatment was looking successful so both mum and my father would be taking the trip from Newport to Catterick, and staying in a hotel overnight. The passing out parade was an amazing day. There were demonstrations on contact drills to showcase some of the skills we had learnt, and also weapon stands where family members could see the many tools of the trade for the modern infantryman.

After the presentations, we all headed to the NAAFI for a pint. We had spent 6 months living together and working together, but this is where we would all part. After saying goodbye to my training buddies, I now had the joy of another 2 weeks leave at home before I would be joining my battalion in Aldershot.

Chapter 5

Soldier.

I SPENT MOST of the 2 weeks back home in pubs and clubs. Although I was still in the very early days of my military career, I felt a great sense of personal pride and achievement, and with the prospect of a possible 22 years to serve, I was going to make the most of it. Joining my battalion couldn't come round quick enough.

The battalion was based at Normandy Barracks in Aldershot, having just moved from Turnhill. I collected my rail warrant and loaded up with my new kit, leaving Newport train station ready for the start of my new life. Once I got to Aldershot, I took a taxi to the barracks.

I couldn't believe it when John Saunders, a lad I knew from school, came out of the guard room to greet me.

"Didn't know you were coming mate!" he said.

He was obviously surprised to see me, although later on, he informed me that there were quite a few lads from Newport on camp. He took me into the guard room while I waited to find out where I was supposed to be going.

Halfway through a cup of coffee, a platoon sergeant arrived and gave me a brief welcome to the Fusiliers before instructing me to grab my kit and follow on.

He led me to the accommodation block, "Ok Spence, you're

going into 4 platoon, B Company. Drop your kit here and sort your stuff out. The rest of the company are out on a speed march, but they won't be long."

While sorting through my stuff, the rest of the platoon came bursting through the door, dripping in sweat. Another lad I recognised from my school years, James Evans, was also in B Company. How many more bloody people was I going to bump into down here? I soon found out that it was quite a few.

I settled into my new home right away, and with the recruit training out of the way, it was more or less like a 9 to 5 job. Unless you were on operations, exercise, or guard duty, you could go home on weekends, and there was far less bullshit.

I'd been in the battalion for a couple of weeks when one day I was making my way into B Company Headquarters and saw something interesting on the notice board. It was a poster inviting people to sign up for a sports parachute course. Ok, it was nothing like the Parachute Regiment do, but it's still jumping from a plane. I thought this was my chance to prove myself to those who had said I'd never make it as a Para because I was scared of heights.

I swiftly added my name to the list.

A couple of weeks later, 4 platoon were being punished on the parade ground because a cigarette butt had been found under a bed during inspection. I was in the middle of being run ragged when a runner appeared to tell me that the Sergeant Major wanted to see me in his office. I walked to his office wondering what the hell I could have done.

"Sir, you wanted to see me?" I said as I stood across his desk.

"Yes Spence, you and Aled have been picked for the parachute course this Monday. Are you still up for it?"

"Yes, sir!"

"Good." he replied.

I was quickly excused from the rest of the hammering my colleagues were enduring and told to get my shit together, and be ready to report to Netheravon Camp at 09:00 the following Monday. And that was that. I could now look forward to 2 weeks' worth of jumping out of aeroplanes. I was thrilled.

Aled and I rocked up nice and early Monday morning to begin the course. It was run by the Joint Service Parachute Centre ("JSPC") and virtually every instructor there had completed a minimum of 1000 jumps with some even reaching 5000. There was a bunch of us on the course, with the majority of lads being Royal Marines.

The type of parachute we would be using was a ram-air design, which was rectangular in shape to make it extremely agile. We would be doing static line jumping, which in simple terms means that the parachute deploys automatically once you jump out of the aircraft.

Our canopy container was attached by a long webbing strap, which was secured to the aircraft at the other end. After you jump, the strap reaches its maximum length and becomes taut, opening the container to release the main chute.

We had at least 6 hours of ground training to cover before we would get the chance to jump as there was a lot to go over; leaving the aircraft safely, what to do in the event of malfunction, the usual safety advice. Most importantly, in the event of an emergency, we were shown how to use the Parachute Landing Fall ("PLF") which is a technique used the world over to minimise risk of injury.

The basics are that you keep your legs together and slightly bent, elbows tucked in, and as soon as you touch the ground, you slightly twist your body, so you fall into a roll. In theory, the kinetic energy will pass through your whole body rather than just your legs.

On the front of the harness were two safety toggles, one to cut away your main chute and the other to deploy the reserve.

We also carried a Cypress, which is a brand of Automatic Activation Device ("AAD"). In the event of malfunction or injury, the job of the AAD is to deploy the reserve chute.

The AAD was pre-set to a height of 1000ft and would deploy the chute should we drop below that range uncontrollably.

Once the instructors were happy with our drills on the ground, it was time for the real thing.

We jumped from between 3500ft and 5000ft out of a Cessna, and it was a good 15-minute ride to get up to jump height. Once the jump-master had checked that we were over the drop zone, he called us over one at a time to the door.

I vividly recall watching each person nervously inching forward on their knees and counting down until it was my turn.

I got myself into position and hovered at the edge, looking down. Even though we'd been told it wasn't a good idea, I couldn't resist. Bloody hell, I wish I had listened.

I plunged through the opening and started going through my drills.

One thousand…

Two thousand…

Three thousand….

Four thousand, Check canopy. I looked up, and everything was going smoothly. I grabbed the steering toggles and tested them…. Left turn…. Right turn…. All good.

Now I was happy, I had to locate the drop zone and aim for it. The canopy had a natural forward speed of about 20mph, so if you had a 20mph wind behind you, it would mean an overall speed of 40mph. I had an altimeter on my wrist, which showed me my height and was used to help you land.

You would land similar to an aircraft by flying into the wind. At 1000ft, you head downwind, at 500ft you head cross wind, and at 300ft, you turn into the wind to slow down the canopy.

As the ground drew nearer, I checked the altimeter. 100ft…. 80ft… 60ft… 40ft… 20ft… 10ft … and flare. I pulled both toggles down firmly, putting the brakes on for a nice two footed landing.

With my first solo jump completed, I felt amazing. Although I was bloody terrified of heights, I had overcome my fear and trusted my life to a little bit of cord and nylon. Back in the aircraft hangar, we watched a video of our jumps to examine any errors and help us perfect our form. I managed a good first jump. My head stayed up, and I demonstrated a good, stable exit followed by good canopy control and landing.

Aled was doing fine as well, and over the next couple of jumps, I progressed to dummy pulls. Dummy pulls are also static line jumps, but while falling, you must simulate pulling a ripcord, usually an old rolled up newspaper. After three successful dummy pulls, you could then move on to free-fall.

Unfortunately, I didn't get a chance to try free-fall jumps as the wind picked up and put a stop to all jumps for the rest of the course. During the 2 weeks, we only managed to fit in four jumps. It would be in Canada the following year before I would get another chance.

Back in Aldershot, the battalion, along with many other military units, were getting ready for a different type of operation. Operation Fresco. The Fire Brigades Union was planning strike action to secure a better salary. The union demanded a 39% pay rise, which would bring a firefighter's salary to around £30,000.

All three branches of the Armed Forces had the task of providing emergency cover if it went ahead. A training plan was put together.

We would have several weeks of training ahead to get up to speed on the equipment and vintage Green Goddesses would be our fire-fighting weapon. The Goddesses dated back to the 1950's and were very basic with no radios, cutting equipment, or power steering. On top of that, with a maximum speed of about 45mph, it could take some time to get to a call out. They could do the job, and after all, the British military is known as the best in the world for getting on with whatever they're given.

We learned about ladder drills, how to connect and hold the hoses safely, and how to use fire hydrants and the external water pump. As for going into buildings, that was a no-go. There wasn't the time or the resources to train us for that. All of the indoor work was left to members of the Royal Navy and Royal Air Force. They provided Breathing Apparatus Rescue Teams ("BART") and Rescue Equipment Support Teams ("REST").

Our team worked well together, and we felt ready, if necessary, to hit the streets. To be honest, it would've been better for all concerned if they didn't strike, although that didn't stop me secretly hoping they did. It was something different, and we trained for it. We just needed the go-ahead. It was eventually confirmed. The first strike would be Wednesday, 13th November.

We loaded up the Green Goddesses and headed for our area of operations ("AOO"). My battalion was assigned to cover central London. Each company was assigned a temporary fire station from locations spread throughout the city. My team would be working from Chelsea Barracks, and split into groups; two day teams and two night teams.

The Metropolitan Police's traffic division was based with us for the duration of the strike to provide us with an escort. They would be essential. We weren't familiar with the area, and if an emergency call came through, we had to get there as soon as possible. There would be no time for maps or a sat nav. We also had a high-ranking fire officer on standby to provide professional advice if needed.

While we were stood down, we made use of the beautiful scenery around Chelsea. Early morning runs around Chelsea Embankment and through Hyde Park were a lot less boring than the usual circuit around Aldershot. I took advantage of our surroundings and did a spot of sparring in the gym as I had recently joined the company boxing team.

The day of the strike arrived and it was planned to last 48 hours beginning at 18:00. This was what I'd secretly been hoping for. This was my shift. At 18:00, we were eagerly standing by in our Gore-Tex, readily waiting for the first call. Twenty minutes into the shift, our first call came through.

An accommodation block was on fire a few miles away, but when we arrived, it wasn't what we were expecting. It was a trainee nursing block, and evidently, some of the trainee nurses thought it'd be funny to set a small bin alight – just to get the Army out. As funny as it might sound, it was a total waste of resources that were already pushed to the limit as it was.

We dealt with way more calls than normal, most of them deliberate and aimed at pissing us off and wasting our time. One that wasn't a prank, however, was an apartment block that was ablaze. There were about five floors and the fire was being contained on the ground floor.

Myself and a teammate stupidly ran into the block and up the stairs to start evacuating the building, banging hard on the doors as we made our way to the top. There was no response. As we headed back down the stairs, we realised the fumes had rapidly penetrated the building, and we were suddenly overcome by smoke.

I understand now just how easily smoke can kill and can honestly say that it was a frightening experience. I pulled my jacket up over my mouth and nose, but the smoke still managed to get in. My eyes were burning, and visibility had disappeared to nothing. I held my back against the wall as I tried to make my way down the staircase. I was only on the second floor and couldn't see anything.

It was such a relief when I felt someone grab me and pull me out. It was a member of the BART team. It was a close call, but my own stupid fault for going into the block when we'd be instructed not to. Needless to say, I kept out of buildings after that.

With the firefighter strikes done and dusted, we had a busy period ahead of us back at Aldershot. I was moving out of B Company and into the Support Company's Mortar Platoon, whilst the battalion was getting ready to move into new barracks.

Over the next few months, we settled into our new digs. Mons barracks, which had just been built a few hundred metres away. We now had single man rooms complete with en-suite facilities. I loved it. You had more privacy, and in the evenings, you could do as you pleased without worrying about anyone else.

Most evenings the lads would hang out in each others rooms on the games consoles or just messing about. I had my TV and PlayStation, but most evenings I was out tabbing alone in the Aldershot training area. I loved to maintain a high standard of fitness.

During my time at Mons Barracks, I had the mortar qualification course to undertake as well as the Regular Radio User ("RRU") cadre. The mortar course was brilliant. We used a 81mm and it was heavy stuff. It consisted of a base plate, barrel and a bipod. When used with the C2 sight, we could fire out an assortment of different rounds to just over 5km. Each mortar group was made up of 3 individuals which each having their own job. We had a bloke to sort out the correct rounds, another bloke to drop the round down the barrel, and also someone to line up the targets using the bearing and elevation on the sight. After the training was finished, we carried out a live firing exercise on Salisbury plain. It was really fast-paced and exciting.

It wasn't long before we had a big exercise to look forward to with 3 months in Canada, beginning in August.

We were going to the British Army Training Unit Suffield ("BATUS"), located in Alberta. I loved the place. It was also the only place I've been to where you could drive for 4 hours and not see a bend in the road. The place was enormous.

For our first 6 weeks, we stayed in a Canadian forces base at Wainwright. It was incredible, a real John Wayne sort of town. We stayed in wooden huts and ventured out in the field during the day to practice some drills before going back to camp at around 17:00 to have the evening to ourselves.

One of the high points of my time in Canada, aside from the training, was the rest and recuperation ("R&R"). We had the best part of a week in the city of Edmonton, so, first thing Monday

Canada 2003 as a member of the mortar platoon. I was 23 and didn't have a worry in the world.

morning, we piled into the coach and headed for the city. Our only detail was to be back at the same point at noon on Friday, have fun, and stay out of trouble.

I was 22 years old and perhaps the first time in my life, I was totally happy. My mother was now in remission of cancer back home. I was in a career of my choice – one I was immensely proud of – and I'd already tried out parachuting and firefighting duties. Now, I was living it up with 3 months in Canada. Life couldn't have been better, and when I got back to the UK, I had the team medic course and a 6-month tour in Iraq to look forward to.

After being dropped off in Edmonton on Monday, there was one incident that had stuck in my mind. We were close to a McDonalds near the drop-off point, so a few of the lads, myself included, headed over for a bite to eat before finding a hotel to stay in.

After we finished eating, we made our way to the Holiday Inn down the road. We put four lads to a room to save money, and save we did. It worked out roughly £50 each for the 4 days, which was a bargain if you asked me.

Two of the boys were picked to go on a booze run as we wanted to have a few drinks in the room before heading to the city's nightspots later on. By 22:00, we were all pissed on Jack Daniels and ready to hit the bars. On the way out, John Saunders and I decided to have another McDonalds to line our stomachs and being the competitive type he took off, hollering that it was a race. Unfortunately for John, I ran like lightning and overtook him quickly.

As I neared the entrance, I failed to notice the large Perspex windbreak around the seating area, and because I was drunk, I was looking through it rather than at it. I smashed face first into the barrier, and the force was strong enough that I took John to the ground with me as I ricocheted off it.

With my nose bleeding and bits of grit in the palms of my hand, I had a quick clean-up in McDonalds before carrying on with the evening. What was the most funny would be that the outline of my face was still firmly imprinted on the Perspex when we returned to McDonalds on Friday for the pick up.

Another great memory of Canada was the visit to West Edmonton Mall. At the time, it was the world's largest shopping mall, and it really has to be seen to be believed. With over 800 stores, a full sized ice rink, water park, and pirate ship, complete with seal shows, this was no normal shopping centre.

Tucked away at the far side of the centre stood the Wild West shooting gallery. A real-life shooting range in a shopping centre. For around £30 you could take hold of a whole variety of different 9mm hand guns and unleash 50 rounds down the range. It is an unbelievable sight when compared to the UK. With the R&R over, it was time to get back to training with a tough exercise at BATUS.

There would be thousands of troops and vehicles screaming over the Canadian prairie in a very realistic battle group scenario. With lasers on our weapons and vehicles, it was like a gigantic game of laser quest.

One evening during the exercise, it was my turn to do radio stag in the command tent. John Saunders was on before me, and around 22:50, he came to wake me up and give me directions. He told me to follow some tank tracks for a few hundred metres, and I will come to the tent. "No problem mate", I said as I set off.

I must have been half asleep as I set off following the track. Before long, there wasn't just one track, but many. Instead of stopping and assessing the situation, I stupidly just carried on walking. I lost count of how long I had been walking, and when I turned around, I had no idea which direction I had come from. Everything looked the same in all directions. There was nothing in sight, and I was just standing alone in the middle of the Canadian Prairie. There was no point in continuing to walk as I'd just make the situation worse.

Although I knew I was lost. I knew my team leaders could find me as I had a tracker on my TES kit. The best thing I could do is stay put and wait. I found a large rock that would protect me from the wind and just chilled out. I grabbed a cyalume stick from my daysack (These are sticks that you Snap thus creating a chemical reaction that develops a bright glow lasting many hours) and put it

Canada 2003. Happy times.

on my helmet so the light could be seen for some distance. I had a quick fag before getting some sleep.

About an hour or so later I can hear people in the distance shouting my name. The search party had arrived as these 5 members started to come into view. Seems I started off walking in the right direction but then went completely off course. Instead of the few hundred metres, I should have walked, I ended up a couple of kilometres away but all was well.

It was a rough old exercise, and it was also the most time I had spent in the field in one outing – 3 weeks. Three long weeks without a decent night's sleep, tasty hot meal, or a proper wash. It really makes you appreciate the small things in life when you return home. The weather was unlike anything I'd seen before. When we arrived in August, it was the same as a good British summer, with temperatures up in the 80's. By the time we came to leave in November, it had dropped to -10, or -20 with the wind chill, and there was about 2 feet of snow. Almost too soon, it was time to leave this incredible country and head home. When we got back, we had a week off and a chance to catch up with family and friends.

Battalion life was fairly quiet until after Christmas, and then the diary was once again full of commitments. There was a hectic 8 weeks ahead because in April, we were heading to Iraq on Operation Telic 4 for 6 months. I just had my team medic cadre to complete, which would be no problem.

I was already planning my life post-Iraq and had decided that once the tour was over, I was keen to attempt the infamous Special Air Service ("SAS") selection course. It was something I'd had an interest in. The biggest disadvantage I had was that on the surface, I was still a fresh recruit and considered relatively inexperienced, having served just over 2 years. What I did have in my favour though, was my high level of physical fitness combined with a rock solid, never quit attitude. I was using Iraq as my first taste of combat and proof that I could stand up to the test of soldiering properly in a real warzone.

In the meantime, training for Operation Telic 4 began in earnest.

Chapter 6

Iraq

PRIOR TO OUR deployment, we had a briefing in the lecture hall with the Operational Training and Advisory Group ("OPTAG") on the pre-deployment training we would be undertaking. This began with a PowerPoint presentation followed by a film showing us the current situation in Southern Iraq, it was a little bit about the daily life but most importantly, the reality of the conflict and the challenges we were likely to face.

The video also contained some graphic images, and to be fair, the pictures were a massive wake-up call. Seeing those images of guys with gunshot wounds, missing limbs, and the possible effects of nuclear and biological warfare, it really made you sit up in your chair and take note of what could be lying in wait.

Our OPTAG training was broken down into different areas and covered all the likely situations we might encounter, as well as the Standard Operating Procedures ("SOP's") to deal with them. We broke off into little groups of around 15 men, and over the period of a week, we spent several hours going over the training.

The first lesson my group had was on the Arabic language, and a friendly Iraqi man in his mid-40s was given the task of training us. They didn't expect us to be fluent of course, but we were expected to grasp some of the basics. Things like how to greet someone and ask a person's name were important, and it also fed into the "hearts and minds" ethos of the deployment. If you're polite and friendly, you may be able to get the locals on your side, and then half the battle is won.

The first phrase our tutor taught us was, "As-salamu alaykum", which means "peace be to you". After hearing it repeated to us a few times, it was then our turn to try. "As-salamu alaykum…As-salamu alaykum…As-salamu alaykum…", over and over, we practised until it was second nature. We then moved on to the next phrase, "Wa-alakum-as salaam", which means "peace be to you also". Again, we went over and over it. It was an enjoyable experience, and after 2 hours, I must have learned ten phrases, a lot more than I had managed after years of studying French in high school.

Further training followed with a lesson on the traditions and practises of the Muslim faith. A big no-no was never to wave or shake hands using your left hand as it's a sign of disrespect. Muslims use their left hand to wipe their arse so you get my point, right hands only. We also had to respect their beliefs, prayer times, and general way of life.

AFTER WE COMPLETED the lifestyle and traditions phase, it was time to get back to the more serious aspect, which was the training that would keep us alive on the ground.

First up was how to conduct a body search for intelligence information or weapons while working as a 2-man team. One man provided cover while the other worked his way around the body, always working from behind to make sure you don't end up with a broken nose from a cheeky knee to the face.

Next, it was vehicle check points ("VCP's") and how to stop, question, and fully search a vehicle, including all the hiding places even the car manufacturers probably don't even know about. There was public order training to follow in case of a large scale city riot, and finally to finish our training to the max came what was probably our biggest threat, that of the IED, the Improvised Explosive Device. The IED can come in many forms, but the three most common methods we were likely to encounter were from the ones carried on a person, a vehicle, or just disguised at the roadside. They had – and still do have a deadly reputation and were probably the last thing you want to experience or come up against.

We studied and practiced the drills for finding a device time and time again, and the plan was simple; depending on the size of the device, we would evacuate the area and set up a cordon as far out as required. Any device around the size of a mobile phone would require a cordon radius of at least 100m, and anything larger – up to vehicle size – would see that cordon stretch out to a considerable distance of 400m. These figures were just for built-up areas however, if it was open ground then the distance was doubled. That's 800m or 8 football pitches if you encountered a car bomb on open ground.

Once we finished our training it was time for one last exercise. We headed down to Lydd on the southeast coast. We used a training area that consisted of a number of buildings in the layout of a village. For years soldiers have used training locations like this to fine tune their skills in patrolling and fighting in close quarters and built up areas, and for us it was no different. The village was presented as a town within Southern Iraq. Loud speakers played Muslim prayer hymns, and mock characters roamed the streets playing the locals. For us, it was a chance to put the skills we had learned during the week to the test, whilst in a safe but realistic training scenario.

When the training was done and dusted, we had a bit of downtime and a chance to spend some time with family and friends before being deployed. I spent most of the time in the Dodger playing pool with John or in the clubs getting pissed. A lot of the lads took out loans to buy themselves some Gucci kit to take away with them, or expensive electronics with laptops being the most popular. What's £500 for a computer when you're on deployment for half the year, you can save a lot of money and more than make up for anything you spent now.

The Saturday before we left, my mother, father, and I headed to The Dodger for the night with a plan to meet up with John later. It might seem strange, but I wasn't nervous or worried about going to Iraq. Perhaps I was a bit ignorant, I'm not sure.

To be clear, this wasn't some act of bravado, I was genuinely excited, and it was the precise reason I joined the Army. It's no different to a runner who spends months training in the early hours of the morning through wind and rain, building up to that one big race. At some point, they just want to run it for real. I felt the same. After months of military training exercises in the UK and abroad, this was my time.

This was my marathon!

That evening in the pub was brilliant, with plenty of drink and a good few attempts on the karaoke, spirits were high. Just as the night was coming to an end, the pub landlord came over and wished John and I a safe journey and promised to have a pint waiting for us upon our return. The last night at home felt like the longest day ever. I wasn't leaving until 22:00 but every time I looked at the clock it had barely moved. My bags were already packed and waiting by the door, and I was starting to feel a bit restless and anxious.

A couple of beers and a few DVD's helped to pass some of the time, and before long, John was knocking on the door. My mother and father waited up to see me off, but I hated goodbyes at the best of times, I would much prefer to have snuck out quietly and avoid all the hugs and best wishes. But that wouldn't be right. Of course, I was a little emotional, and dare I say it, I had a tear in my eye as I said goodbye to my parents.

I had a couple of hours' kip in the car on the way back to Aldershot, and after the weekend I'd had, I certainly needed it. As soon as I got back to camp, I jumped straight back into bed. I knew my uniform needed ironing, but that could wait until morning. Most of the expensive stuff in my room, like the TV and PlayStation, had been put into storage until I returned, so I drifted off to sleep listening to the radio on my Nokia phone. I managed just a couple of hours of sleep before I was back at it and starting to get my shit together.

I was only packing a few luxury items to take: a disposable

camera, my Sony CD player, some photos, and a hip flask given to me by my sister which she had gotten engraved for me. The flask had brandy in it, and even if I didn't drink it, it was comforting to know it was there. The coaches were lined up on the parade square and had been there for the last hour. The amount of kit I was taking was going to require two trips to the coach. I had my Bergen, daysack, chest rig, as well as my body armour and my holdall containing all of my personal stuff.

All our weapons had already been sorted out. We lined up in platoon order while a final kit check was done; documents, MOD90 (army ID card), dog tags, and passports. I grabbed my CD player from the holdall before jumping on the coach.

We were flying from RAF Brize Norton on a Tristar, and the flight was going to take approximately 8 hours with a short stop in Qatar. As soon as we landed in Qatar, I could already feel the heat penetrating the skin of the aircraft, and the moment the doors opened, it felt like you were walking into a sauna. It must have been in the high 90s, and within 20 minutes of being on the ground, I was starting to feel dizzy and needed some fluid quickly. Mercifully, there was a fridge stocked full of litre bottles of water, so I grabbed a cold bottle and necked half the lot in one go. The symptoms quickly dissipated, and I began to feel better just in time for our call to board the next flight.

The flight into Basra was on a different aircraft, a Hercules transport aircraft. This flight was the less comfortable of the two but was fortunately the shortest. As we approached Basra, a call came over the speaker telling us to close all window sliders and fasten our seat belts. Then, unlike normal passenger planes, all the aircraft lights were turned out, sending us into complete darkness.

The reason behind this was that if someone wanted to take a shot at us as we came in to land, having the lights on display just screamed, "Here we are! Come and shoot us!". Turning out the lights minimises the risk to some degree, although there is little you can do to mask the roar of an aircraft as large as a Hercules dropping out of the sky.

When we landed the first thing I needed was fags as I had run out in Qatar. I could see a little shop inside the arrivals lounge so I grabbed my luggage and ran over quickly before we were called in. My first impression of Basra airport was that it looked amazing. It was immaculate, and the floor was highly polished marble, far more luxurious than anything I had seen in the UK. In the shop, I found a young lad no older than 15 years of age running the place.

The shop was filled with Iraq memorabilia, and of course, countless brands of fags. I asked the boy how much they cost and he said they were $7. Although this was Iraq, we used American currency which was great due to the exchange rate. It worked out at about £3.50 in British money whereas 20 fags back home cost more like £6.00.

I said, "I'll have a pack of B&H please". To my surprise, he threw me a pack of 200. I told him that I only wanted a pack of 20, only to be told that it was $7 for the whole carton of 200 cigarettes. I couldn't believe it, what a bargain! I ended up buying 1000 right there and then.

Our call came over to get ready to move. Outside the airport, there must have been about fifteen coaches waiting, so I grabbed my Lionel Richie CD from my holdall before chucking it back in the luggage space. I was pretty relaxed on the journey to Shaibah logistics base (SLB).

We arrived at SLB at 01:00. We were absolutely knackered and wanted to get our heads down, but there was a load of admin to carry out first. It was 04:00 before we finally got to bed. Waking up the next morning, the sun was shining, and we were given a tour of the camp.

The place was huge with thousands of troops based there. It served as the main operations base for the south and was the Iraq version of Afghanistan's Camp Bastion. Everyone would spend time here before they were deployed on the ground. It was relatively safe and secure and allowed us the chance to acclimatise before hitting the streets.

There were shops to buy fags and other bits and pieces, as well as a large tent which contained the entertainment stuff like Sky TV, games consoles and telephones. Over the far side was the field hospital.

Conditions at SLB were pretty good, but I was only there a few days before it was time to move on to our Forward Operations Base ("FOB"). My team's support company would be based at Az Zubayr port ("AZP"), Bravo Company would be at Camp Chindit, which was also in Az Zubayr town, and Alpha Company at Amarah to the north, with the other company's scattered at various other places.

AZP was pretty basic. We stayed in a large air-conditioned tent, which was more like a sauna due to our tent having the broken air conditioning unit. There were ten beds to each tent with wash rooms and toilets close by. The heat was relentless. You could take a shower at 02:00 and walk back to the tent with just a towel around you. The heat radiated from your skin, and you'd be completely dry after walking 100 metres or so.

The scoff house was just a stone's throw away and stocked with all the usual stuff we had back home. Hand hygiene was on top form as there were a number of anti-bacterial gel machines stationed at the entrance to the restaurant along with 10 gallon barrels of mineral water.

In support company, our role during the tour was to help train the current Iraq police force. We were supported in our role by a member of the British Military Police and an Iraqi interpreter.

It was more or less a 9 to 5 job with no night shifts required. Each morning, we would have a quick kit check before loading up into two Snatch Land Rovers. We were given our plans for the day, a packed lunch, and 6 litres of water that were issued to each man.

We had a number of different police stations to visit throughout the day, and just getting to each one was a risky task in itself. We always tried to change the route we took to the stations, as well as varying our arrival times. The terrorist groups knew we visited the stations during the day, but we needed to keep them guessing. While we could change our route around the city, what we couldn't change was the route back to AZP.

There was only one way in and out of AZP. Unfortunately for us, the road was about a mile long with open ground on either side. It was a dangerous road but we had no other choice but to use it.

During the drive out, your arse cheeks would be so tight that you could hold a penny between them.

While the Land Rover would provide some protection against small arms fire, if we were hit by an RPG we would be done for, and in all honesty, a whopping great Land rover isn't exactly the hardest target to hit.

Once we arrived at the police station, we would quickly get ourselves into a solid, all-around defensive position. Damo, the red cap, and the interpreter would spend an hour with the Iraqi police going over skills and drills.

Some of the stations were right in the centre of the city, and we needed eyes in the back of our heads if we were ever going to spot a real threat. There were hundreds of people who I thought looked dodgy, and the chances of spotting a car bomb were slim to none.

The roads were packed with cars, bikes, and even donkeys. There was no sense of road management, and everyone was treating the road as if it belonged to them. It was like the Arc De Triomphe but with far less driving proficiency.

While we were providing protection, we daren't stand in the same spot for more than a few seconds. You just didn't know if anyone had you in their sights.

As for the Iraqi police, the most professional thing about them was the way they maintained their patrol cars. They might as well have been brand new they were so shiny and dent free. It's a shame the same couldn't be said for the people driving them. They seemed far too laid back, given the ever-present risk of death that surrounded them.

On several occasions, I had seen loaded AK47's left in unlocked patrol cars while the officers disappeared into the station for a coffee or prayer. It's pretty unbelievable. The condition of the cells was equally as bad. I'd seen a few with as many as ten people crammed into it. There were signs of human faeces up the walls, and the place was buzzing with flies. It looked more like a torture box than a cell, I wouldn't have kept animals in conditions like that, let alone human beings.

So far on the journeys between stations and the port, we had encountered very little drama. I can only remember one time when I thought it was really going to kick off, and that was while I was on top cover in the Land Rover.

We were making our way through some back streets when a young child no older than 10 years old started shouting "Ali Baba… Ali Baba!" and pointing down the road in the direction we were headed. Ok, I thought, time to get ready for a contact.

If they hit us with an RPG though, were finished. Thankfully, it didn't escalate any further that time. We might have been having a peaceful run around, but word on the street was that Alpha Company was having a fair few contacts up North in Amarah. During our patrols, we often visited Bravo Company at Camp Chindit for a coffee break.

Camp Chindit was a decent size for the company, with the Iraq Police Training Academy situated adjacent to it. Every morning, a large number of Iraq police recruits made their way to the academy for their day's training. The training academy even had instructors from the Metropolitan police teaching there.

It wasn't long before the decision was made for us to move from AZP to Camp Chindit. It was easier, safer, and less for us to travel each day. I was more thankful that I would be out of that sauna of a tent we had been staying in.

We moved into our new accommodation late on a Tuesday evening and only had time to dump our kit before it was time for us to turn in for the night. Another busy day ahead tomorrow.

Chapter 7

The bombings.

WEDNESDAY 21ST APRIL

I WOKE UP at around half 6. The sun was already shining and it was starting to warm up. Even at that time in the morning, the temperature was in the high 60's. I really thought it was going to turn out to be a good day. Little was I aware of the danger that was looming in the distance.

After getting dressed, I went to the cook-house to get a fried breakfast down me and chatted with the lads about our plans for the day, most likely deliberating over which DVD we should watch that night. Our team leader, Damo, came in and said, "Lads, be outside the Ops room at 08:00 for a sitrep and a quick kit check".

I quickly returned to my room to sort my shit out and pack away any unnecessary kit, and at 07:55 I was stood outside the Ops room with the rest of my team mates including Chris Bennett, Danny, Chris R and Steve Hallett, or Big H as we called him due to his stocky frame.

Damo filled us in on the police stations we'd be visiting today and gave us a current situation report on what had been happening overnight before moving on to the kit check. We had all our kit laid out in front of us, and he started calling out the items. Body armour and 2 trauma plates, helmet, personal role radio (PRR), 10 rounds of 5.56 ammo, dog tags, 1 morphine auto injector, and a full CamelBak. Our food and water had already been loaded onto the snatch Landrover.

All of a sudden, it sounded like the loudest noise I have ever heard, followed by a huge vibration through the ground.

What the fuck was that, I thought.

I began grabbing rounds of ammo and stuffing them into my pocket, then along with the others, I legged it into the nearest building for cover while we waited for more information. I had loaded the magazine with ammo faster than ever before when a runner came in just as I was finishing putting the trauma plates back into my body armour.

He said, "Reports are saying a suicide bomber has driven through the camp main entrance, we have a number of dead and many injured. Are there any medics here?"

"Yes" I said, "I'm a combat team medic."

He said, "Ok, grab your kit and follow me".

Everyone in the British Army, from a pastry chef to a paratrooper, is trained in basic first aid as part of their recruit training, but a team medic undergoes a more advanced programme of an additional week. It covers areas such as gunshot wounds, broken bones, hot and cold injuries, and administration of IV drips and the triage of patients.

I positioned myself just inside the compound as the injured were brought in, some by foot, some by Land Rover. The injuries were shocking as men soaked in blood with deep shrapnel wounds came into the building.

I could see one bloke holding his hand in pain, and I called him over. He had lost part of his hand and fingers but I didn't have any proper medical kit with me apart from a load of FFDs (first field dressings. These are a highly absorbent sterile dressing with tape to secure it in place), all I could do was wrap the dressing around his hand as tightly as possible to reduce the blood loss.

My responsibilities quickly changed when a large crowd of

people began to gather outside the camp entrance. There were perhaps 100 or more who had heard the explosion and had come to see what had happened. This was concerning the camp commanders as it made it much more likely that we would become a target for a second attack now there were more people here.

My team were given the task of dispersing them, but it was going to be risky. We had a number of guys from B Company who were going to provide armed cover for us from within the compound, but being on foot outside the compound, we would have little protection against a vehicle bomb. As we advanced towards the camp entrance, we got down low and used the Hesco bastions for protection. Hesco bastions are a type of military gabion that provides defence from explosions. They are usually filled with heavy material like rubble or earth and are made from collapsible wire and heavy-duty fabric.

The Iraq police overlooking the remains of the first suicide bomb outside Camp Chindit. Photo courtesy of Mike England .

Lieutenant Lake turned to us and said, "Right lads, just remember your spacing and prepare yourselves for some graphic scenes".

As soon as we started to run out, I could see what he meant about the graphic scenes. There were blood stains smeared along the walls, human body parts sprawled across the floor, and brick walls reduced to rubble. The Hesco bastions had shrapnel sticking out of them, while some had even begun to fall apart. There were also the remains of the bomber's vehicle.

A car crusher couldn't have twisted the vehicles metal into the shapes the bomb had created. It was barely recognisable as a vehicle except for the odd buckled wheel.

I was taking in the realities of the situation faster than a Pentium processor as I hurriedly made my way towards the assembling crowd. Tensions ran high as we formed our baseline spread out over a distance of 70 to 80 metres and faced the crowd. Some of the horde were getting aggressive towards us with some of them throwing rocks, and I could feel the build-up of sweat starting to run down my forehead. I was the last man on the far left with Chris Bennett to my right, Lieutenant Lake, the next man down, and Chris R, big H and Danny to the far side.

An elderly Iraqi man approached me with tears in his eyes. He had two young children with him, a boy and girl no older than 9 or 10, and was desperate to get past me. Why, I didn't know, I couldn't understand him but thought perhaps his son was a member of the Iraqi police and was worried about his safety.

I had my orders though, no one to break the line. I did allow him and the children to pass me, but only to sit on a rock to rest just a couple of metres behind me. It had been an hour or so since the bombing and most of the crowd had left, leaving 30 or 40 people. Unbeknown to me, something else was about to happen.

I could hear a vehicle engine in the distance that sounded like it was high revving. I started scanning the ground ahead of me. Where is it, What is it. I couldn't see anything but didn't need to wait long. A vehicle appeared from the buildings about 200 metres to my front, and it was heading directly towards me.

Oh, shit. I lifted my rifle up and looked through my sight. I knew for sure that it was another suicide bomber. It didn't take a genius to work that out.

Could I hit it. Unlikely, I could barely even see the vehicle through my sight as it bounced all over the place. Even if I did manage to hit it, it wouldn't make much difference because the bomber was going to die anyway and would carry on regardless of any injuries or damage to the vehicle I caused. Plus, it could have been remotely detonated.

In those vital few seconds, I decided that time spent trying to shoot the vehicle would be time wasted. I had 2 choices. I could either go to the ground where I was, but risk being run over, or I could get as much distance between myself and the bomber as quickly as possible.

I choose the latter. I could see what looked like a shell scape about 30-40 meters away, and it soon became a race against time. To make matters worse, I'd been having problems with my left knee recently, which made running painful, but at that moment, it didn't hurt at all.

I started to sprint as fast as I could towards the ditch whilst trying to keep the bomber's location in the corner of my right eye. I stopped a few metres short and looked over my right shoulder. I could see the vehicle passing within 20 feet of me, and I thought I was safe.

At that moment, he detonated the bomb.

There was a colossal explosion followed by a feeling that can only be described as being hit in the back with a sledge hammer. Immediately after the deafening boom came an immense blast wave; a huge amount of pressure lifting me up and slamming me into the ditch.

I ended up lying face down with my rifle blown clean from my arms and the sling wrapped around my neck. I couldn't breathe. The impact had knocked the wind out of me completely, as if I'd just been rugby tackled by Jonah Lomu running flat out into me. My back was hurting, and I wasn't sure if it was broken, although it felt like it was.

The remains of the second suicide bombing. The one I was wounded by

Photos courtesy of Mike England.

At first there was total silence, but this soon turned to screams as people started to take stock of the situation. My radio came to life. It was Chris Bennett...."Neil mate, are you OK?"

I said, "Yes mate, but I think my back is broken".

I tried getting to my feet, and it was then that I noticed my arm. The blood was squirting out all over my clothes. My left forearm had been torn open by shrapnel, and there were bits of flesh hanging out. When I saw the state of my arm, I began to flap and felt faint. I grabbed my field dressing and tried my best to tear it open, but with only one arm working, I couldn't do it. I needed help, and quick, I was losing blood.

My ears were ringing and there was dust all around me. I wasn't sure if it was a good idea to try and run across the waste ground but I had no choice. I had to make a run for it.

Grabbing my rifle in my right hand as I held the field dressing between my teeth. I ran towards Chris, who had made it safely to another ditch. I gave him the dressing and showed him my arm. As he applied the dressing, I could feel myself becoming weaker as shock started to take over. I'm not sure who it was, but someone came up behind me, lifted me up, and said, "Run".

I headed towards the camp and the company aid post and felt like a complete mess. My left knee was in agony, my back was pounding and sore, my left forearm was literally torn open, and I was covered in blood. Strangely, although my arm was by far the worst injury I had, it didn't hurt. It might have been the fact that all my nerve endings had been damaged, I'm not sure. It just felt heavy, really heavy.

As I neared the camp, I passed the bombers' truck. It had been blown into two parts, and a male body was lying just a few feet away. No, it wasn't the bomber. It was a member of the crowd. He couldn't get out of the way fast enough and didn't stand a chance. I stopped to look at him. He had lost two limbs and part of his face and was very badly burned. I remember thinking, that this chap would of been walking around only a few minutes ago and now look at him. It was an image I would remember for many years to come.

I soon had two medics running out towards me, and they helped get me to the company aid post. I lay on the floor with a pillow beneath my head and was jabbed in the leg with pain relief, good old morphine. There was another lad in the room being treated with me, Lance Corporal Williams, and he had taken shrapnel to the face. I wasn't sure how bad it was, but the amount of bandaging on him showed it was more than just a nick. We made eye contact, and I just gave a little nod.

Chapter 8

Coming home.

AT LAST, THE morphine was starting to kick in, and I was beginning to feel more relaxed. There was also this overwhelming sense of euphoria that followed, a feeling great happiness of at last conceding to my situation. My mind was racing. Holy shit. Did that really just happen? Stuff like that only seemed to happen in Hollywood movies. Although I was rather unhappy about my new chest rig being cut apart when I was being treated, I could always buy another one.

I was shepherded into a medical Land Rover which was taking me to the field hospital at SLB. My arm was now raised above and behind my head, out of my sight. Still, I had no pain, just a deep ache and an immobile arm. I thought shit, my arm is dead. I asked the medic by the side of me how it looked, and her reply was, "I'm no doctor, but it sure looks nasty". At the last minute, it was deemed too risky to travel by road, so a helicopter was ordered instead. I was happy with this, always a fan of flying. Within 10 minutes, a Chinook arrived and landed just outside the back of the compound. I was rushed out and up into the air in no time, with the on-board medics monitoring me throughout the flight.

We arrived in what seemed like minutes and dropped down right outside the hospital entrance. I was taken out on a stretcher and left waiting behind the helicopter. The sun was shining, but it was uncomfortable, I could feel the heat from the Chinook's turbines blowing towards me and my now wasted arm. I remember thinking, if this takes any longer they'll be treating me for burns as well.

After a few minutes of roasting in the heat, a team of medical staff took me into the hospital. There must have been about ten of them in all and it was like a scene from the TV programme Holby city.

Lying in the emergency room, I hear the medic updating the emergency team. This is Neil, a P1 casualty. He was injured an hour ago in a bombing. He has a shrapnel wound to his left forearm and is complaining of back pain. Unsure of any other injuries at this point. Morphine was given at 09:55

The emergency team started cutting my clothes off me, and I see the mask placed over my face. I'm soon under anaesthetic. I woke up about 4 hours later with a huge bandage on and feeling very sweaty. It was mid-afternoon by then and the temperature was in the high 90's.

A friendly nurse came over and said, "Neil, your parents have been informed of your condition, and you'll be leaving on the next medical flight back to the UK". I knew my arm was bad, but I didn't expect to be sent home. The nurse helped me to the showers to get cleaned up before my transport arrived. While in the shower, I finally got to see what the blast had done to my back. It was black, a deep bruise now covering most of it.

The bruising was most likely caused by my trauma plates; solid pieces of steel that are fitted into the front and back of your body armour to protect your heart. After having a good scrub and feeling much fresher, I made my way to the TV room to see some of the news from back home, and a few hours later, the transport came for me. There were four more injured lads coming back to the UK with me that night.

We grabbed all of our kit and left to board the minibus that was waiting for us outside. The journey to the airport was slow and unnerving as we passed the many VCP's along the route. We travelled under armed escort with military Land Rovers to the front and rear, filled with guys armed to the teeth, on guard for any potential threat towards our soft skinned minibus. However, I was unarmed, and even if I did only have the use of one arm, I still would've felt safer if I'd have had a firearm on me. You know, just in case.

Each vehicle coming towards us put me on edge. After all, the last vehicle I saw heading in my direction only 12 hours before had nearly blown me to bits. Despite my apprehension, we made it to the airport without any difficulties, and straight away, I was made to feel at home.

We were housed in a building on the side of the airport in an old aircraft hangar. There was tea, coffee, and hundreds of DVD's to watch, and we also had the use of a satellite phone to contact family and friends. We were then informed that we would be leaving later on that evening. I called my mother who told me the military had contacted her shortly after the bombing to tell her that a few members of the battalion including me had been injured, but they weren't told much more at that point.

She also said that the bombing had made the front page of the South Wales Argus, our local newspaper. She supplied them with an old photo of me, along with what little information she'd been given about what happened. After our conversation, I got some food down me while I waited for the flight.

Due to undisclosed reasons, the flight was going to be delayed by 48 hours. The real reason was because of the appalling availability record and repeated breakdowns of RAF aircraft. So, all we could do was make use of the services on offer to pass the time. I lost count of the number of films I watched, most of which, surprisingly, were war films. Two days later, the plane was all set, and I was strapped into the aeromed flight for the 8 hour trip to Brize Norton. From there, a minibus would take us to Sellyoak hospital in Birmingham.

It was a good job I was shattered as there was no entertainment on the flight, and the only view I had was of the ceiling. I was secured to the bed like something from Silence of the Lambs with only a nurse popping back and forth for company. I must've fallen asleep before we got to maximum altitude because the next thing I remember is being woken up just before the start of our descent. The flight had at least given me some much needed rest. Clutching our kit, we saw the minibus waiting for us outside.

Selly Oak hospital has now closed down, but back then it was home to the Royal Centre for Defence Medicine ("RCDM") and they had an entire ward dedicated to treating injured service members. It was also one of the best trauma hospitals in Britain at the time. There were people there with just about every battle injury you could think of. From gunshot and shrapnel wounds to burns and amputations, this place had seen it all. It's no surprise that many army medics spent time here before deployment to conflict zones; they could gain the most paramount of experience.

My parents were at the hospital by the time I arrived, and I was given a bed straight away. A nurse told me I'd be going into theatre later that day, and she wanted to change my bandage now. "Yes, that's fine" I said. It was starting to smell a bit by this point. What should have been a simple task became a nightmare taking nearly an hour. The nurse tried to remove the dressing, but it was too painful, so she gave me a shot of morphine and soaked the bandage in water for 20 minutes.

She came back a bit later and started to cut through the layers of cloth. The last few were unbearable, and I asked her to stop.

She said, "It has to come off Neil."

My reply was, "I'm well aware of that, but it hurts."

She disappeared, and a new nurse turned up, a more senior one, and in one quick motion, she ripped the bandage off.

"OUCH." I shouted out.

I nearly hit her. What we didn't realise was that my arm had been left with an open wound, and as she was removing the dressing, she was, in fact, pulling out the guts from inside my forearm. Due to the 48-hour delay of my flight, the blood had congealed, and the tearing had re-opened my injury. Boy, was it painful. Anyway, it had at last been changed and so I waited to be called for surgery.

I finally got taken down to be operated on and was out for only

2 hours. Apparently, there was a problem. Because my arm had been left exposed, it was now badly infected, and the repair work couldn't go ahead.

The surgeon removed the grit and shrapnel that was embedded in the wound and stitched my arm up. I was given a strong course of antibiotics to kill the infection and told it would be a few weeks before I could return for the repair work. My back was still bruised and sore, but it would make a full recovery. My arm, however, was different. I ended up with 100% ulnar nerve and deep tissue damage. The ulnar nerve runs from the elbow through your arm and allows your little finger and ring finger to feel sensation. Both fingers were completely dead.

I hadn't yet been told when I could go home, so most of my time was spent outside in the smoking shelter talking to the other guys. I was a heavy smoker and could get though a good 40 fags a day, which also meant forty trips in the lift. I could've used the stairs but I was still connected to an IV drip.

Talking to the other lads, we traded stories. You could tell that many of these men were deeply traumatised by their experiences, and I couldn't blame them. One lad I was talking to had been in the back of an armoured personnel carrier when it was hit by an RPG. He had taken quite an impact and most of the shrapnel as well by the look of him. He had staples from head to toe. He looked a right mess. There was also a young soldier in the bed opposite me, he was 19 years old and had taken a round from an AK47 straight into his forearm. Believe me, the lad was in pain, and there was very little flesh left on the bone. One thing was for sure, many of these soldiers' lives would change forever, some for the better. Most for the worst.

After 4 days of bumming around, I was told I was well enough to go home and could be released into my parent's care to recover at home. I was then placed on long term sick leave by the military doctors. My uncle was also on his way up to visit me, which was great, and even better, that once he arrived, I would be going back with him. After packing up my kit bag and saying my farewells to the lads and hospital staff, I got in the car and headed for home.

Taking the more scenic route home along the M50 and A449, I had never before been so happy to see the sign, "Welcome to Wales". As soon as I returned home, friends and neighbours popped in to see me, and it was great to see everyone, but what I really wanted was to pop to the Dodger for a nice cold pint of Guinness. I hadn't had one since the night before leaving for Iraq, and it was something I was very much looking forward to.

Chapter 9

I'm Maria

IT WAS THE day after I was released from the hospital, and it was exactly one week since the bombing. I decided to venture out into the city nightlife. In hindsight, it wasn't the best idea given my current physical condition, but it wasn't as if I was going out on my own. My buddy Dave was coming along too.

I'd had a good few Jack Daniels' by the time we headed into town, taking in a few of the bars along the way before ending up in the city's main hotspot. I was on the dance floor with a pint of Guinness in hand while Dave went to the bar to get another round in. Without warning, a punch lands cleanly on my face. Almost dropping to the floor, I stand back up, and people are just dancing around me like nothing had happened. I could feel the blood dripping down my chin, so it was time to leave.

Whilst trying to get out of the packed club, I bumped into Dave, drinks in hand.

"What the hell happened?" he asked.

"I'll tell you tomorrow mate." I replied, as I made my way out and disappeared to go home.

The blood kept flowing so I stopped at a kebab shop and grabbed a wad of serviettes to plug the wound. When I got home, I could see the damage; my top lip was split wide open. A long time ago, as a young boy, I had been bitten on the face by a German Shepherd, leaving two slice marks in my lip. The bite had healed well, but this punch had opened up the old scar, and it was clear that a trip to A&E was needed.

On arriving in A&E, it was evident that the night was in full swing. The place was packed with drunks full of alcohol-fuelled bravado. After a quick check-in with the triage nurse and labelled as "walking wounded", I took a seat and waited to be seen, getting all the entertainment I needed to pass the time from the drunken louts littered about the waiting room.

A short while later, a nurse called me into a cubicle. The look on her face when she saw me was a picture. I looked a right mess. My nice crisp white shirt was now covered in a mixture of Guinness and blood. My top lip was sliced open, and my left arm had a thick bandage on it.

"What on earth has happened to you?" She asked.

"I was punched in a club an hour ago" I replied.

Although she had probably worked that out for herself. What was puzzling her was my arm.

"What about your arm?" she asked.

"Oh," I replied, "I was blown up by a bomb last week."

To be honest I'm not sure if she wanted to laugh or cry, but I'm certain that our exchange would have stuck with her and made her shift a change from the usual happenings found in A&E on the weekend.

The nurse did a great job repairing my lip, and I was soon back in action.

For the first few days back in the UK, I mooched around the house, mostly getting in my mother's way. I spent wasted hours browsing the internet looking at random stuff while I waited for the pub to open. Then, I would disappear until dark.

I wasn't drinking heavily but made sure I paced my consumption to fill the day and keep myself occupied. It was a coping mechanism, my way of dealing with the stress of the bombing and my now large surplus of time. I used to play darts years before joining the Army, and being sat in the pub all day, I quickly took it up again. I played all day from the time they opened until 21:00, stopping at 13:00 for lunch – a juicy 8oz sizzling steak complete with all the trimmings. This became my routine, exactly the same every day as clockwork.

The South Wales Argus was keen to hear my side of the story, so a reporter and photographer were sent to interview me. The article made front page news and began to attract a great deal of attention. Before long, the BBC also got in touch. Radio Wales and Radio 5 Live also wanted to meet me and do an interview about the bombing, which wasn't a problem. However, Radio 5 Live wanted to do the interview from my home.

They set up a huge satellite dish in the back garden. The neighbours must have thought we were trying to recreate a scene from the film ET. Aside from the dish, another issue was that because this was going out live, I needed to be careful of what I was saying. I didn't want to be responsible for breaking operational security or the Official Secrets Act. As a private soldier, it wasn't up to me to determine what's important and what isn't.

They told me the interview would last no more than 10 minutes, and I would be asked some questions about the bombing and what daily life was like on the ground in Iraq. They were also interviewing former SAS soldier and best-selling author Andy McNab about his new book, and as soon as his interview was over, it would be my turn. The questions ranged from how I felt about the war to how the locals treated us and, of course, a number of inquisitions on the bombing itself. After the interview, I was given a taped copy as a keepsake.

Another strange sequence of events had taken place. This went back to the beginning of April, and just after I deployed to Iraq. My parents had been doing some shopping in the city centre, and while walking through the carpark, my father noticed a Porsche Boxster with a cracked rear plastic window. He got out a business card from his wallet and left it on the windscreen.

Later that day, he received a phone call from the owner asking if he could book the car in for a replacement. The car was booked in for Friday, the 23rd.

It was on the Wednesday before that I was wounded.

On the Friday, the Porsche owner didn't turn up for his appointment. My father wasn't too concerned as he was already planning to visit me on Saturday morning at Sellyoak hospital so he could have done without the job anyway.

When my father returned to work on the Monday. He received a phone call from the Porsche owner to apologise and said he was called into work at the last minute and asked if the car could be booked in once again. It was, and this time, he turned up.

Over a coffee, my father asked what his job was, and he replied, "I'm a pilot with the RAF. I'm currently working aero med, bringing wounded soldiers back from Iraq and Afghanistan."

My father said, "My son was injured in Iraq on the 21st and flew back on the 23rd, the day of your appointment." It turned out that he missed the appointment as he was the pilot who brought me back to the UK that Friday night. It's a small world, and more so as my father was also working on a vintage car at the time that belonged to Sir Geoffrey Inkin. A former Commanding officer of the Royal Welch Fusiliers, who was later the chairman of the Cardiff Bay Development Corporation.

About 10 days after the bombing, letters of best wishes started to arrive from my mates still out on the ground in Iraq. I also received a card full of messages from the lads. One, from a good friend Paul Baston, read: "All the best Spence. That's one war wound to add to the many more to come."

It was a welcome reminder of the great yet darkly tinged humour shared by those in the forces. Included in the well wishes were some letters from my company commander, Major Nick Lock. There were two letters, one addressed to me, the other to my parents. The letters outlined exactly what had happened that day and how proud he was of the men under his command. The thing is, I could remember exactly what happened that day. It was so fresh in my mind that I could taste it.

The following week and being a glutton for punishment, I went back to the club, only this time I ended up being the aggressor. I was on the bottom dance floor alone and quite drunk when another drunken lad knocked into my bad arm. I instantly lost control and found myself grabbing him around the throat before tripping him up. Before anything else could happen, four burly doormen grabbed me and ejected me from the club. I found myself sitting on the curb alone and started to cry. I didn't understand what or why, but something inside me had changed. I was becoming angry, and another month passed without any update on the repair work to my arm.

Soon, the BBC got in touch with me as they were running a documentary series called "Real Story" that was being presented by Fiona Bruce. The episode was entitled "Coming Home" and examined the provision of treatment for wounded service members returning from Iraq and Afghanistan. Because my aftercare package had failed, I was invited to appear on the show, and after meeting with the recording team and doing some fancy editing, the episode would be aired towards the end of November.

A couple of months after the bombing I was out drinking. I was alone in Yates when I saw a girl on the dance floor. I made my way over and had a bit of a dance and a chat. Her name was Maria. We spent about an hour together before she took my number and said she would meet me later as she was on a girl's night out.

Later that night, my phone was ringing. It was Maria, but I decided not to answer it. I thought she probably just wanted me to pay for her cab. I went back to Yates the following Saturday, and there she was, out with her friends again. She noticed me and walked over.

She said, "My friends say I shouldn't be speaking to you as you let me down last week."

I apologised, and that was that. We become almost inseparable. She was 23, the same age as myself, and she lived in Bettws with her mother and younger brother. Maria worked at a local electronics factory near Cwmbran and also the chip shop part-time in the city centre. I spent every night with her at her mums place.

She left the house every morning at 07:00 and wouldn't get home until 16:30, so when she went to work I would catch the 06:55 bus from Bettws to Newport city centre. Each morning without fail, I bought breakfast and a coffee from McDonalds before walking to my parents' house where I would stay until Maria finished work.

Every evening Maria would cook my dinner, usually a fry-up and we'd end up just watching TV upstairs while having a few drinks. One night while at Maria's, I received a phone call to say I was AWOL from my battalion and that if I didn't return by midday the following day, the Military Police would be sent to pick me up.

I explained that I had been injured and was on long-term sick leave, but as far as they were concerned, they were just following orders. Early the next morning and still only having the use of one arm, I dragged my kit to Newport Army careers office to get a rail warrant, and 2 hours later I arrived at North Camp station for the trip to Aldershot. From there, it was a mile and a half walk to the battalions barracks.

As soon as I arrived, I dumped my kit and made my way to see the Regimental Medical Officer ("RMO"). Needless to say, he was shocked that I had been ordered back given the condition I was in, and wrote out a sick note before sending me traipsing back home again.

One evening Maria and I were playing pool at the Globe Inn, in Maindee. We had been together for only 10 weeks when I thought, I want to marry this girl. Over the next few weeks, I got some cash together and went to buy an engagement ring, intending to propose as soon as possible. I didn't want to rush into things but I had no choice as my battalion were due to deploy to Cyprus for a couple of years once they returned from Iraq, and at that time the future of my military career was uncertain. If I stayed with my battalion while I was single, I would go alone. However, if I was married, then marriage quarters could be arranged for me. If Maria said yes, then the wedding would have to take place before the Cyprus deployment.

We ended up going for a few drinks in Yates. I had the ring in my pocket and dawned on me that I had forgotten her surname.

Yep. I'm about to purpose to this girl, and I couldn't remember her last name. A stroke of luck as she pulled some items out of her handbag, including her passport.

"Let me see your passport photo?" I said.

She passed it across. I only wanted to see what her surname was. Yes, I remember that now. We carried on for a few more drinks in town before heading to my regular curry house. Towards the end of the meal, I asked her to marry me, and she said yes.

I was again ordered back to barracks and, this time, managed to stay a week, but only just. There was hardly anyone around, so there wasn't much to do as my TV and PlayStation were still locked away. It was incredibly boring. I went to my room and found that a new

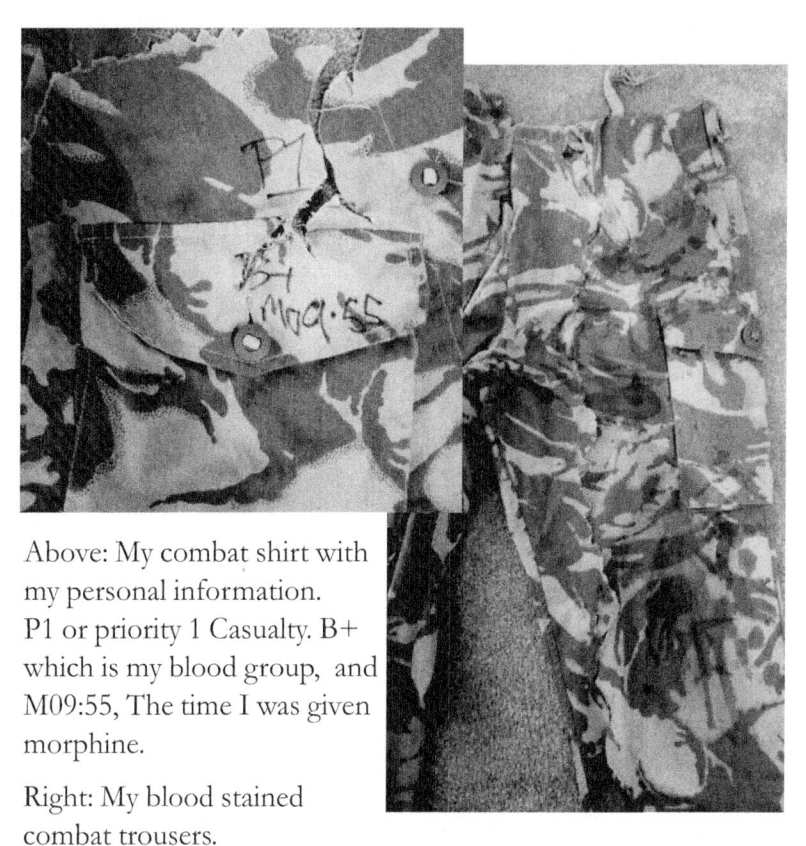

Above: My combat shirt with my personal information.
P1 or priority 1 Casualty. B+ which is my blood group, and M09:55, The time I was given morphine.

Right: My blood stained combat trousers.

lad had settled in, which was a bit of a shock. My personal belongings had been moved into the block upstairs, and this lad had taken my space. I couldn't say anything to him. It wasn't his fault. It just happened from time to time.

My new room was completely empty except for my MFO box sat in the corner. I opened it, and right at the very top was my pair of desert combats, the ones I was wearing when I was blown up. I suddenly felt angry, I couldn't believe what I was seeing. I don't know what came over me, but I started to punch the hell out of the box.

Once I had calmed down a bit, I took the clothing out to have a closer look. My shirt and trousers were cut into pieces, and the blood stains were still very much visible. On the top left pocket of the shirt, my details were still clearly written:

P1 (priority 1) Casualty
Blood Group B+
M (Morphine) 09:55

I didn't even know they existed. I thought they would of been thrown in the trash. They would eventually become of sentimental value and something I couldn't part with.

Being stuck in camp was horrible, I was medically downgraded, and the only thing I was practically allowed to do was breathe. I didn't want to be there on my own, I just wanted to be back at home with Maria. The thing is, I was still in the military and, therefore, had to be in a military establishment. However, I had a plan to rectify that. The RSM was back in the barracks carrying out some admin so I paid him a visit to express my concerns.

I asked if I could be posted at the Newport Armed Forces Career Office as it would be a win-win situation for me. The Army would still be in control of what I did, and I'd only be working a few miles from home, so it was perfect. The RSM asked me to come back in half an hour, and he would see what he could do. He agreed to my request, and true to his word, he made the necessary arrangements. After a quick phone call, he sent me over to battalion HQ to collect a rail warrant so that I could report to the careers office at 09:00 on Monday. It was brilliant news.

I arrived in smart combat 95 uniform on Monday morning to meet the recruiting team. There were four platoon sergeants working there; one representative for each of the four Welsh regiments. The recruitment officer from my battalion was Sergeant Neil Williams. There was also a Sergeant major from the Royal Green Jackets who was in charge of running the place.

It was an enjoyable place to work. The office was open from 9 till about 4:30, and while I was expected to work those hours, most days I was on my way home just after lunch. If I wasn't sent out on the bacon roll run, I would be walking the streets of Newport handing out leaflets to anyone who looked close to enlistment age. By this time I also had daily physiotherapy at the Royal Gwent Hospital on my hand. So 2 hours of the day would be spent there having ultrasound therapy.

One morning, just before leaving for the office, a brown envelope was delivered. It was from the Army Personnel Centre in Glasgow, informing me that since my discharge from Selly Oak Hospital, I had been under the command of Y List. The Y list was a unit for injured soldiers who aren't well enough to return to their parent units or are likely to be given medical discharge. They would have

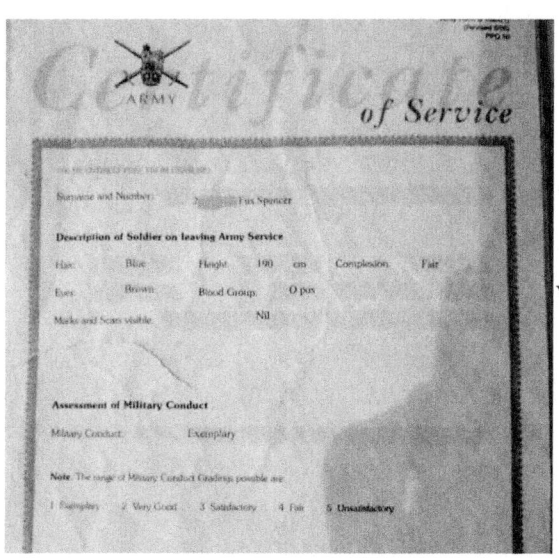

Just adding insult to injury. My service record with all the wrong information.

been responsible for all of my treatment and general well-being.

This explained it. My lack of treatment and AWOL status now made sense. I was lost in the military system.

It was now October and 6 months since the bombing. Maria and I hosted our engagement party at The Dodger, with the wedding to follow not long after as it had to come together so quickly before Cyprus. I wanted to wear a No1 Dress blue military parade uniform but didn't have my own set as they were very rarely issued. I was going to have to beg, borrow, or steal if I wanted to get married in a set.

Raglan Barracks was only a couple of miles away, and I knew a few of the TA lads who worked there. I thought I could ask whether there were any uniforms I could use. Unfortunately, they didn't have a full uniform for me, though I did manage to come away with some trousers. Sergeant Williams was heading back to Aldershot in a few days and offered me a lift. With a bit of luck, they would have some uniforms in camp. Thankfully, they had the rest of the uniform, which was a relief, and one thing ticked off the to-do list.

Maria and I visited the church to book a date for our wedding. St Johns in Maindee. It was also the church my parents got married at. After going through the diary with the priest, we settled on Saturday, 18th June – just 10 weeks away.

There were so many things to organise in such a short period of time, but Maria's mum kindly organised most of it. Over the next few weeks, we had our banns read and enrolled in a marriage preparation course. Every Wednesday evening for 90 minutes, we went through the program with other couples preparing to tie the knot. It was all starting to come together.

We even managed to book our honeymoon online at a bargain price of £500 each for 10 days all-inclusive in Cabarete in the Dominican Republic. It was all going so well.

The wedding was now just 10 days away. It's early evening at Maria's house and my phone starts ringing. It was my father.

He said, "I've got some bad news. Your mums in hospital. Her hips have snapped, and it's unlikely she can make the wedding."

It was too late for me to see her now so I arranged a visit the following day. When I arrived, she explained what had happened. They had spent the afternoon in the city centre doing a bit of shopping and decided to pop into the pub for a quick drink before going home. While they were walking back, her hip collapsed.

She was unsure what the problem was with her hip or how long she would be in hospital but from where I was standing I had my doubts as to whether she would be out in time for the wedding. My mother was determined to be there.

With everything in place, it would be too late to cancel, so I just had to hope and pray that it would turn out ok.

The next time I was at the careers office, I asked if I could finish a week before the wedding as I still had a few things to do. Sergeant Williams checked with the RSM back at Aldershot, and it was approved.

My mother soon found out that the damage to her hips was due to Osteoporosis.

Two days before the wedding I heard a knock at the door, it was Sergeant Neil Williams and he had come bearing gifts. He'd polished up a pair of ammo parade boots for me to wear. They were so highly polished you could've seen a spot on your face when you looked into them. I hadn't asked for the boots. It was just a kind gesture on his part and very thoughtful of him.

The night before the wedding I stayed at my best man's house talking about old times over a few drinks, and a curry.

The day of the wedding was bright and clear, and you could sense that it was going to be a warm day. Sadly, my mother was still in hospital and had asked the doctors if she could be allowed to attend the wedding in a wheelchair. The request was declined, but they did agree to let her leave the ward for some photos later in the day on the hospital grounds.

As per the forecast, it turned out to be the hottest day of the year, with temperatures reaching the 80's and with my uniform on it felt a lot hotter. I still felt really smart in my uniform though, despite the fact that I didn't have a medal on display.

The church service went smoothly, and we had some lovely photos taken outside and at Belle Vue Park. Afterwards, we went across the road to visit my mother in hospital where a nurse had helped her get into the dress she'd bought for the special day. It was an uncomfortable situation as I was both happy to have her taking part in the proceedings, but sad that she couldn't enjoy the whole day with us. You could see the sadness in my mother's eyes as she missed her only son's wedding. She would've done whatever it took to be at the church, but what the doctor says goes.

Later that day I went back to my parents' house to get changed into more comfortable clothes. Jeans and a shirt ready for the evening party that would take place at the Merry Miller in Bettws. My father only stayed at the party for a short while as he wanted to be with my mother, and I totally understood that. I can't help but think how sad it must have been for her alone at the hospital and missing out on my day.

Once the evening party had ended. A number of us headed back to Maria's mum's to continue the party. It was so warm that night, as we drank champagne and looked through some of the photos that guests had taken. There would be no sleeping on my wedding night though, as my uncle was going to be picking us up shortly for an early morning flight from Manchester.

As soon as I arrived at the hotel I gave my parents a ring to find out how things were. All was well, and we got told to just enjoy ourselves. The Dominican Republic was a great experience with amazing weather and soft sandy beaches. There was so much for us to do, including a vast array of water sports and day trips.

We did pay for one day trip, and we bypassed the outrageous prices the resort were charging, by going with independent group offering the same tour. It worked out at around 70% cheaper, while offering the same experience.

Travelling by Jeep, we went into the mountains where we learned how they made Jamaican rum and Cuban cigars, before being taking to a restaurant for lunch, and afterwards we were taken to a special place they had in the hills.

It was a bit of a walk up some hilly terrain, before we arrived at this lagoon of clear blue water that was surrounded by mountains on all sides. It was like something from the film the Goonies, with rock slides etc.

When we finally returned home, my mother was still in hospital. Altogether, she was in for 5 weeks.

It wasn't long before I moved out of my parents' house and into Maria's home with her mother and brother. I wanted to give my parents some space as they needed it now that my mother had been discharged from the hospital.

As she could no longer climb the stairs, my father shifted the bed downstairs and also installed a ramp in the rear garden so she could enjoy some time out there. It must have been an incredibly difficult experience for my father juggling the care of my mother as well as trying to keep his car upholstery business going.

A few weeks after the wedding I was invited to attend a medical board assessment to decide the outcome of my military career. My mind was all over the place and I was under a lot of peer pressure from family and friends who thought it would be for the best if I left the Army, and I could see where they were coming from.

Firstly, I had been blown up by a bomb, and I might not be so lucky next time. Secondly, my mother's health at the time meant that the family could do without any more bad news, and thirdly, it was looking unlikely that I would be returning to my previous military role. I was heading towards more of a desk job and I knew that wasn't for me.

I told the medical board about my family situation and my current feelings towards the military. I didn't want to work behind a desk, and if I did remain in service, then I wanted to go back into a combat role.

Ultimately, I left the decision in their hands.

In the meantime, life continued as before. I was still working in the career's office and Maria had started working full time at the chip shop in the city centre. I also found out that my mother didn't have osteoporosis. It was much worse. The cancer had come back, and she would be starting treatment shortly.

It was early evening when once again my phone started ringing. It was my father letting me know that my mother would be going to St Anne's Hospice tomorrow. I should point out that I really didn't understand much about cancer, I saw it as more of a treatable illness than a deadly disease.

The following day, I took a trip up to the hospice to see her. I grabbed some magazines from the shop on the way there, things like "Take a break" and "Bella" were her favourite, hoping that at least this would keep her occupied until it was time for her to come home. She seemed ok, conceding to the situation and telling me she was going to the hospital on Friday for her medication. I left St Anne's trying to remain as positive as she was.

Outside the hospice my father told me about something that happened just a few days before. It was a sign of what was about to happen. My mother had been lying on the bed in the living room just reading a magazine, while my father was in the same room doing some business work on the computer. All of a sudden, a white Dove, and as white as can be, came flying into the patio doors at speed.

He jumped out of his chair to see it surprisingly still alive. He showed me the picture he took of the smudge mark that was left on the glass. You could see everything. The beak, and even the bones in the wings. It was remarkable that it was still alive. The following day it flew away.

It was just over a week since she was admitted to hospice. It was early Saturday morning, as my father phoned, telling me to get to the hospice as soon as possible. Maria and I got there within 20 minutes. My mother's condition had deteriorated dramatically, and I was told that she was unlikely to last the day. I was confused, I thought she was getting better. It turns out that he thought it would be better to keep the real situation hidden, and now I could understand why.

I wanted to go into the room to see her but I had a bad chest infection at the time so I asked the nurse if they had a mask I could put on, as I didn't want to pass my germs to my mother and make things worse. I was told to just go in.

Other members of my family were dotted around the room while she slept soundly due to the amount of medication she was on. She looked so incredibly weak and fragile. She must have been half the weight she was just a few days before, and the colour had drained from her skin, leaving her sallow faced.

I asked my grandmother when she was likely to wake up, only to be told that she wouldn't. This was it. Now, it was just a matter of time. I wondered if she could hear what we were saying, I don't know if she could. My sister and brother-in-law would want to be here too, but they weren't answering their phones. He asked me and Maria to go quickly to Bettws and bring them back so my auntie gave us a lift.

We finally managed to get hold of them, but by the time we got back, it was too late. We ran through the hospice entrance when Dave came over, his face giving away the reality of the situation. She was gone. I felt like I'd just been hit in the face with a brick. Dizzy and weak, I couldn't even cry. The feeling was horrendous, and my mind was in overdrive.

Straight after, I went outside with Maria for a smoke. My grandmother came over and said, "I think you and Maria should move back in with my father that night as he would need the company."

The suggestion riled me a bit. It wasn't about the need to look after him but why we had to be the ones to move in. She was aware that I had enough of my own problems going on. With the suicide bombing, my career, and being newlyweds. From my perspective, there were other family members who could have helped, and once again, the burden was put on me. Despite this, I agreed to move back in. I put my cigarette out as the family was going to the hospice chapel for some prayers and a few minutes to think of my mother.

There were about 10 of us in the room when a family member said the Lords prayer, and this was followed by a few minutes of silence. Then something awful happened. The song Ding-dong the witch is dead from the film, The wizard of Oz came into my head, and I couldn't control it. I had no idea why I had these thoughts, but the more I tried to not think about it, the worse it got. It was like a battle between good and bad was taking place inside my head.

Looking around at the other family members with their eyes closed and deep in thought. Although I had no idea what they were thinking, I wouldn't have imagined they would be thinking anything like I was. I was riddled with guilt over these thoughts and didn't tell a sole. I knew they wouldn't have understood.

She passed away, Saturday 1st October 2005, aged just 48.

At the Royal Gwent hospital with my mother and father on my wedding day. It was the last photo I had taken with my mother. She passed away 15 weeks later.

Chapter 10

Mum's gone

As soon as we returned home I went next door to tell the neighbours the sad news. The neighbour and her family had been good friends with my mother for over 20 years. It was distressing for everyone who knew her.

The next day, my father, Maria and I, didn't have a clue what to do with ourselves. It was almost like it was a dream – it couldn't be real, but it was.

The TV was never turned on, just the music player. The music playing at the time was by one of my mother's favourite singers, Barry Manilow. The album was played repeatedly over and over and over again. I didn't like the music but my mother did. She used to play his album day in, day out, and I guess my father must have felt like she was still around when the music was playing. I thought, well, if it helps him, then by all means, let it play.

My father found the whole grieving process to be tough. It wasn't just the traumatic experience of losing his wife, but he also had the financial pressure of being self-employed.

As well as having to take time off work to care for my mother while she was ill, he was also trying his best to hold his business together. Most people struggle to do one of those things, let alone both at the same time, but he was – and still is – a strong man.

I was still riddled with guilt over the thoughts i had in the hospice chapel and still kept them to myself. I had an idea that would put my mind at ease.

I decided to write a letter to my mother explaining that I didn't mean those thoughts and had no control over them. At least this would give me some closure. The plan was to drop it in the coffin when I went to the funeral home.

The day arrived to visit mum. She looked at peace and had been gracefully dressed, but it was still something I never wanted to see. After a few minutes with her, I gave her a kiss before dropping the letter down the side of the coffin.

On the morning of the funeral, I was running around like a headless chicken, making sure we had all the food sorted for the wake.

There was a knock on the door, and I opened it to find Carol, the landlady of The Dodger pub. She had the boot of her car full of food all readily prepared for us. It was a true act of kindness.

The funeral took place at St John's Church. Just 16 weeks before I been there on the happiest day of my life getting married, and now I was back there on my saddest. The funeral for my mother.

The church was packed, and there was a huge mixture of people she had known. A group of Asian lads who lived in the community even came to the service to pay their respects.

When the funeral was over, there was a lot of tension hanging in the air. The TV was still off, with only the music in the background to mingle with the strain everyone was feeling. Both myself and my father were stressed out. It had been a rough few months, even years, and slowly, we were starting to clash. I'd lost count of the number of arguments we had, and it was the last thing we wanted at that particular moment.

A few days after the funeral. Myself and my father decided to pop to town for a few drinks. Leaving late afternoon, we lost count on how many drinks we had, but on the way home, I suggested that we pop into the Riverside Tavern as we were passing.

After a couple more whiskeys, it was time to leave. Outside, my father failed to see the steps and went crashing to the ground, ripping his jeans in the process. After making a few weird noises, he said, "I didn't see those steps on the way in."

I replied, "That's because we didn't go in that way, you stupid bugger."

After getting him home and into bed. I grabbed some frozen peas from the freezer to put on his bruised knee and left him to it. When I went in to check on him the following morning he was green. He was covered from head to toe in peas as the bag had burst, and he looked like a ninja turtle.

It was about 2 weeks after the funeral, and a letter came through the post. It was the outcome of my medical board meeting. I was to be medically discharged on the 8th of January under the term, ceasing to fulfil army medical standards. My discharge was just 3 months away.

I phoned the army careers office and told them about my medical discharge, and they said I didn't need to come back to the office now, and that I could remain at home until my discharge date.

I had mixed emotions over the decision. I was disappointed because my career that I worked so hard for now over with just 3 years and 360 days service, but happy that I could now move on with my life. With mum's passing, being a newly wed and all the troubles of the past year. In honesty, my heart was no longer in the military.

With my military fate now sealed. Me and my father went to Maindee for a pint. Sipping away on his pint, he turns to me and says, "Why don't you just come and work with me."

I said, "Why not. I've got nothing else to do." And that was that. I would now start learning the trade of a car upholsterer.

Despite the fact we were working together, the arguments at home still continued. Me and Maria had also just got ourselves a dog of someone who had to give it up. The dog was a year old. A wirly ginger patterdale that was called Taylor, but we soon changed the name to Jasper.

It was now Christmas day. Almost 3 months since she had passed and another paranormal event took place. My father was doing the dinner. His first time ever I believe. Some other family members were also around, and Maria and I were sitting at the dinner table. I look across at the patio doors and see the smudge mark that was left from the doves' impact shortly before she went to hospice. Despite my father trying his best to remove it, the smudge remained. But there was something else I could see. This was on the left side glass, and it was an image I had seen before.

The day after boxing day, I took a trip to Warren James, the jewellery shop in the city centre and was gobsmacked. The image of an angel I had seen on the patio door glass was identical to the one that was on the necklace I had brought from the shop for my mother's birthday, shortly before she passed. I have no explanation for this, and it still baffles me today.

After 3 months at home of almost constant arguments, I had had enough, I didn't want any more fighting. It was time Maria and I had a place of our own. We took a trip early in the morning to the council housing office to see what our options were. After an hour of waiting, we were finally called in for a chat. I knew that if I was totally honest about living with my father, then the chance of us getting a house or flat would be zero. I basically told the housing officer that I was ex-military and now homeless (at least the first part was true).

After what seemed like hours, we were offered a place at a homeless shelter until a property became available. Of course, I rejected this, I couldn't take up a spot in a shelter whilst knowing there were genuinely homeless people who needed it more than me. Once we completed the paperwork, it was just a waiting game. I remember thinking, as soon as I'm presented with their first offer, I'll take it.

That evening at home we didn't mention anything to my father about our plans to leave, I just thought it would be better to play it by ear. It was only 2 weeks later when the council contacted us.

Mr Spencer? We have a property that has become available if you're still interested?"

Damn right I was still interested!

"Ok, well, it's only a 1-bedroom flat in Bettws…" she said.

"What road is it on?" I asked, excited.

"Leach Road." She replied.

Maria was thrilled as it was barely 300m from her mother's house. We would be mad to turn it down.

She said "You can view the property tomorrow if you like."

From the outside, it was no oil painting, and the interior wasn't much different, but it was our own place, and it's what we made of it that counts. The housing officer went through the terms and conditions of the property and showed us the inventory.

She then informed us that pets weren't allowed.

No pets? Damn. She hadn't mentioned it before. I'll just 'forget' to mention Jasper.

The council gave us a voucher worth £60 so we could decorate the place, but there was a catch. It could only be used in one store in town which had very little in the way of quality items. Tins of paint for £2 and rolls of wallpaper for £3, you wouldn't find any of your Laura Ashley quality in that place.

Armed with my new tins of paint and multiple rolls of wallpaper, I was looking forward to getting stuck in and making the house our home. I had never put up wallpaper before, so it was a learning curve, and I actually surprised myself. Ok, so there were a few bubbles hiding underneath once the wallpaper was up, but they soon dispersed overnight.

With the painting done and the walls covered, next to come was the furniture which came in the shape of several flat packs from Argos and left me £450 lighter in the pocket. This was going to be another learn-as-you-go job as I'd never put one together before. Two hours later, and with the help of a power drill, it was all assembled. Some people might hate flat packs, but I started looking for more to build.

We had been in the flat for a few weeks when a letter came through the door. It was addressed to me with a military stamp on the front and had been sent from my old battalion. I was invited to a medal parade and a ceremony to celebrate St David's day. It was going to take place on Tuesday 28th February as the Regiment had decided to celebrate the national day early due to plans to merge with the Royal Regiment of Wales on the 1ˢᵗ March – which is the actual date of St David's Day.

Once amalgamated, they would become one regiment called The Royal Welsh. Therefore, the 28ᵗʰ February 2006 would be the last official day in The Royal Welch Fusiliers' 300 year history.

Even though I had been out of the military for 2 months, I was invited to be part of the day's celebrations, and of course to receive my Iraq service medal with the rest of the regiment. I was told I could travel up the night before and stay in the barracks. This allowed me to have a few drinks with the lads in town the night before. Well, there was no way I was turning that down.

I decided to leave mid-afternoon as I could get to Aldershot by 15:00 and have plenty of time for a piss up with the boys. Maria was going to spend the night at her mum's with the dog because she didn't like to be alone in the flat. If you had seen the place, you would understand why.

My mate John Saunders said I could crash in his room for the night, so I dumped my kit and had a quick shower before chucking on some fresh clothing and heading out for North camp. I loved it. It was also a break for Maria whilst giving me the chance to catch up with old friends. Something that is special within the military is that it doesn't matter how long it's been since you've seen each other. You just carry on from where you left off. After God knows how many pints and games of pool, we grabbed ourselves a kebab from Belly Busters before making our way back to the barracks.

On the morning of the parade, I was up early and had a banging headache. I needed a shower and some painkillers. As I made my way towards the NAAFI, the Regiments' adjutant called me over. The adjutant is an officer who is usually the rank of Captain or Major and assists the Commanding Officer with staff duties.

He said, "I've been unable to locate your Iraq medal."

"Really sir? I'll come and take a look." I replied.

I started rummaging through the box of medals but could find none with my name on it.

Bloody hell! This could only happen to me, I thought.

The adjutant tried to reassure me by saying, "I will personally make sure your medal is delivered to your home address within the next 6 weeks." I couldn't say any more to that.

During the parade, I stood in line with the other lads who'd been wounded or were receiving bravery awards. I was presented with someone else's medal for the purposes of the parade, but I would have to return it afterwards. We spent the rest of the afternoon in the officer's mess drinking brandy and talking to the lads about their bravery awards.

I must admit, I did feel a bit of envy. I felt I should have been given a bit of recognition. After all, I had run forwards to treat injured people without hesitation or care for my own safety. But here I was, struggling to even get my basic deployment medal. I felt disgruntled by the whole thing and just wanted to go home.

Back home, my relationship with my father was improving now that we didn't live together, but something in me just never felt right. I didn't suffer from nightmares or flashbacks, but I always felt on edge, like I was constantly waiting for something bad to happen. I was unsatisfied with nearly every aspect of my life. I had a chip on my shoulder and became angry with life.

It had been over 6 weeks since the medal parade, and still, my medal hadn't turned up. I decided to give the medal office a ring to find out what was going on and was told that no one from my battalion had applied for my medal, and the case was closed.

"What the hell does that mean?" I asked.

"You have to apply for it yourself. I'll send some forms out to you." The Lady said.

The forms arrived a week later, and I had to fill in my life story. They wanted to know everything about me – name, army number, and dates of deployment. Every damn thing. I filled it out and sent it off.

I quickly received their response. "Sorry Mr Spencer, you don't qualify as you didn't meet the required deployment duration".

Are they taking the piss? I replied to the letter stating that I had been medically evacuated after being injured in a bomb blast, and

My Iraq deployment medal with my father's name on it.

therefore, I qualify.

A good number of weeks dragged by when finally, a little white box came through the post. I couldn't believe my luck. It was my Iraq medal. Except it wasn't. It didn't have my name on it but my father's initials. I couldn't believe how I was being let down so badly. I got back on the phone to the medal office to explain the error.

"Sorry Mr Spencer, send it back, and we will correct it".

"Forget it, I've waited long enough for this one, I'll put up with it" I said.

More nonsense followed. My service leaver's book arrived. This big red book contains your service history and personal information. I was listed as having blue hair and brown eyes. Well, that was clearly the wrong way around. My height and blood group were wrong, and under the section listing scars, it said "nil". Really? Did they forget about the shrapnel in my left forearm?

As this was an official record of service, it added insult to injury. The military had always spoken about attention to detail, yet they couldn't even get my medal or paperwork correct. It just added to my resentment.

It had been 10 months since mum passed, and dad decided to put the house up for sale. It just wasn't the same now that Mum wasn't around. Within a matter of weeks, a buyer came forward, and the house was sold.

I offered to help my father with the move, and there would be lots to get done. We spent a good few days clearing out all the stuff he no longer wanted. Lots went in the skip, while other bits went to charity. The attic was by far the biggest challenge. It was full of stuff that had been up there since they moved in almost 26 years ago.

On the day of the move, it was upsetting to see the house so bare. To many people, a house is just bricks and mortar, but I've never seen it that way. I've always had a deep emotional connection with places that I've spent time at.

This house was no different. It had been my family home for over 25 years. That's 25 birthdays and 25 Christmas mornings. It was a place where I cried as a bullied kid and a place where I smiled when I was about to get married. It was place I lost my virginity and a place I returned to as a wounded soldier. But it was, unfortunately, also the place where I watched my mother fight her battle with cancer.

With the house now all clean and empty. My father said, "Come on, let's just go."

I said, "Wait, just give me a few minutes."

I started upstairs and spent a few moments in each room. I was mentally thinking back to all the things I'd experienced in those rooms over the years. Both good and bad. I could see myself crying in the bathroom because of the school bullies. I could see my mother in the kitchen preparing the Sunday roast, and I could see the living room covered in paper and presents on Christmas morning.

After I'd been to every room. I met my father at the front door. "OK," I said, " We can go now"

He soon found himself another place to stay. A tidy two bedroom home in Ponthir. It was just a few hundred metres walk to his workshop, and he had the Star pub on his doorstep. I helped him move in and within a week he had a nice tidy set-up.

My family was hit hard again when my grandfather passed away following a short fight with pancreatitis. His loss wasn't just hard on me, but my father's too. In the space of 2 short years, he had to deal with his son being blown up and almost killed, the death of his wife, and now his father. How he was still holding it together was beyond me.

After my grandfather's passing, I became more aggressive. I was slowly losing everything that meant something to me, and I had no control over any of it. At home, the bedroom door was knocked clean off the hinges, and almost every wall had a hole in it. Straight after these violent outbursts, I was filled with huge feelings of guilt. I'd sit in the corner and cry, unable to explain why or what had made me explode. I knew I needed help.

I began by going online to find other soldiers who had gone through similar things to me and found that a great deal of them were suffering from PostTraumatic Stress Disorder ("PTSD"). I didn't know much about the illness at the time but found that many of the soldiers suffering from PTSD had seen some horrific things and were experiencing a lot of the same symptoms I displayed. I noticed that a few of them had been in contact with a military charity called "Combat Stress", so I decided to investigate a bit further.

I checked the charity out online, and after reading about them and what they did, it seemed like they were the people who might be able to help me. It took a while for me to build up the courage to get in touch with them because I was embarrassed about phoning up and admitting I had a problem I needed help with. Yes, I needed help with my mood swings and anger issues, but I didn't like to think of myself as having a mental health problem. It's those two words "Mental Health", it makes you feel like a nutter or psycho and to be labelled as either one was the last thing I wanted.

My doctor had previously prescribed me the anti-depressant Citalopram, but I'd never taken a single tablet for the very same reason. I thought of antidepressants as being for people who were mentally weak – another thing I didn't want to be labelled as. After a few weeks, I finally pulled myself together and got in touch with the charity. They sent out some papers for me to fill in, like my basic personal information, my military service, how I felt day to day, stuff like that. It also had to be signed by my doctor. I completed the form and posted it off right away.

An area welfare officer made contact with me a couple of weeks later and asked when I was free to have a chat with him. I said I was available at any time, and a week later, he came to see me at home. He was a former military man himself in his 50's, well aware of the countless problems that ex-service members face. The conversation started by going right back to the very beginning as he asked me about my childhood. We moved through the different stages of my life before progressing onto more recent matters and what had happened over the past 2 years. We talked for about 45 minutes, during which he simply listened and took notes while I spoke.

It felt nice to talk to someone who listened and understood instead of giving me the usual negative response I'd been accustomed to getting from others. Afterwards, we shook hands, and he said he'd be in touch soon. "Here's my card, any problems just give me a ring". I felt as though a weight had been lifted from me, I wasn't fixed yet, but I had made a start.

Sometime later, I received a letter saying, "Dear Mr Neil Spencer, we have a space available for 1 week at our treatment centre in Newport, Shropshire. Please respond with your decision". They enclosed some documents for me to sign, including a consent form, allowing them access to my medical records. I signed everything and immediately sent it back in the post.

I couldn't wait to get there, but a few days before I was due to leave, I started to panic. I had seen the film "One flew over the cuckoo's nest" a few years before and was beginning to think I would end up in the same situation. I envisioned myself going in with anxiety and coming out with a ton of mental health problems and a daily dose of drugs. Of course, this was all down to my twisted thinking at the time, and it wasn't like that at all.

When the day arrived for me to go to the treatment centre I was looking forward to it as a whole, although I would really miss Maria whilst I was away as it would be the longest we had ever been apart. When I reached the centre, a friendly care worker welcomed me and helped me check in before showing me to my room. Upon entering the room, the first thing I noticed was a Bible by the side of the bed. Is it that bad here that I need a Bible? I wasn't one to read books, let alone the bible. I just don't have the patience. I have never been religious as such but have always believed in a form of afterlife. The amount of strange experiences that had happened over the years left me with no doubt. As for the whole heaven and hell, and a man in the clouds. That I wasn't so sure of.

After unpacking my clothes I took a short walk around the centre to get more of a feel of the place. I couldn't believe the number of older veterans who were there, and it soon became clear that even at the age of 27, I was one of the youngest people being treated. Most of the men were around 50 or 60 years old, with some even older than that. Nearly all of the guys suffering from PTSD had served in Northern Ireland or the Falklands War.

The centre had a beautiful garden area with plenty of benches to relax on. While outside having a smoke, I got talking to a chap who was a former platoon sergeant in the Parachute Regiment. He started telling me about his time in the Falklands and how the lasting mental scars had caused serious damage to his career and family life. The next thing I know, he breaks down into a sobering wreck right in front of me. I didn't know what to say, what could I say? As a young fusilier, I used to idolise platoon sergeants like they were God. They were the ones you turned to for experience, help, or support, and yet here I was in a position to offer help.

I met another bloke who also served in Iraq. He was a bit older than me, and most of his time there was spent in the field hospital, treating the injured. He had 6 hard months of service, and when he returned, he didn't have a mark on him. However, the experience affected him so much that he filled his bathtub with bleach and scrubbed at his skin until it was raw. He may have been physically fine, but deep down, he had some long-lasting psychological issues.

There was an interesting chap who I never got the chance to speak to. He was a strong looking bloke who had served in the Royal Marines and the elite SBS, and he certainly looked the part. He was very quiet, stood over 6 feet tall, and had a tailored moustache.

During the day, I never saw him move from his preferred chair except to make coffee or go to the toilet. He would simply sit there watching TV all day. On my third day at the centre, I noticed this SBS guy wasn't sitting in his chair like he usually was. I asked some of the other lads where he was, and they told me he was in his room where he would stay until he left in a few days' time. I thought this was odd behaviour until I found out why. He lived alone in a bedsit somewhere down south and lived like a recluse. When he visited the treatment centre every 6 months for 2 weeks, he treated it like a holiday. It was his respite, his chance to taste what normal life felt like with people he could empathise with. He apparently found it too difficult to just up and leave the centre on the pre-arranged date to go back to his lonely bedsit, so instead he would gently reintegrate himself back into his regular mentality by spending the last few days at the centre as he would at home. Alone.

It was a good break for me too, I felt totally relaxed during my time at the centre, and for the full week, not a single drop of alcohol ever came close to touching my lips. Unfortunately, as was the same for everyone else, it was soon my time to leave and return to reality. I packed up my belongings and bid farewell to the lads and welfare staff, just in time as Maria and my father were only a few minutes away. It was amazing to see them again, and on the way home, we popped into a country pub for a pint and a catch-up.

They wanted to know how the week had gone and if I felt any benefit from it. The answer was a confident yes. I didn't realise at the time that it was only a temporary fix. When asked if I would like to return, I should have said yes. During that week I had time to focus solely on myself, de-stressing and talking th rough my problems while I had the breathing space to do so, but I was never going to be fixed in just one week. It could take months or even years before I got the full benefit of treatment.

At the workshop, unless something was booked in, we treated Saturdays as our own admin day. A chance to give our cars a good clean, inside and out. We would only work till lunchtime, then normally we'd pop up the cemetery to visit Mum and drop some flowers.

On this particular Saturday, something strange happened. We were heading to Christchurch cemetery and driving up Belmont Hill when I told my father we should leave the car outside and walk through. The reason being, my car had been making a few loud noises, and I hadn't had a chance to get it looked it. I didn't want to drive through in case a funeral was taking place. Just out of respect.

I parked the car on the bridge, and we walk through the cemetery gates. To my left is a large wastebin that's overflowing with flowers, etc. I then see a lone card lying against the wall. It's about 10 metres away. For some strange reason, it feels like I'm being pulled towards it. Just like putting two magnets close together. I felt this invisible energy urging me towards it.

I walked over and picked it up. It was a card that had been left by a family member on my mother's grave for almost a year. I showed my father and he too was shocked. Mum's grave was about 150 metres away as the crow flies and there were hundreds of graves in between. The card could of blown anywhere, but on this particular day it was just lying there. Waiting for me to pick it up. On any other day, I would have probably missed it.

Chapter 11

The break-up

THE FREQUENCY OF our arguments escalated, and soon Maria and I were fighting daily. We were both under massive strain, but I also felt riddled with guilt. I had become so aggressive and angry I hated it, I hated myself. Maria was going on holiday soon with her mother and aunt to spend 2 weeks in Tenerife. I hoped that the time apart would give me some time to unwind and do some thinking.

The day Maria left for Tenerife I was upset, but luckily, I had Jasper, my trusty dog, for company. I didn't have much to do around the house, so I often kept myself occupied by popping around to my father's workplace with the dog for a few hours. It was during one of these visits that I came up with the idea that I'd had enough of the marriage, and as soon as Maria returned, I would let her know how I was feeling.

Now that I had come to this conclusion, I became anxious. How would I tell her, and what do I tell her.

Her uncle dropped them off at Bristol airport, so it was my turn to do the airport run for their arrival home. I set off early as I didn't want to be late. I got there in plenty of time, not least due to the fact that the plane was running a little behind schedule. Before long, I could see the passengers making their way through the arrivals lounge.

I watched Maria coming towards me, and she looked great, wearing a nice dress which showed off her lovely tan. She came running up to me and gave me a big hug, telling me how she had had a fab time but was looking forward to getting back home to spend time as a family with me and Jasper.

Then she reached into her bag and pulled out a gift. It was a bottle of Aramis Life, my favourite aftershave. My heart sunk. I'd already made up my mind, but how on earth could I tell her how I feel now?

During the journey home, I carried on normally as I didn't want to break the happy mood. Once we got back to Newport, I dropped her mum and auntie off first, and it was almost time for me to break the news. There was no easy way for me to do it; I had to come straight out with it. The moment we walked through the door, I asked her to sit down. No messing about it, I came straight out with it.

"I don't think the marriage is working anymore, we need to call it a day." I said.

She began crying almost instantly, asking me if this was really what I wanted and telling me she married me for life, but I was resolute. The atmosphere changed immediately, and I felt a huge load had been taken off my chest. Amidst all the thoughts going through my head, I didn't realise that this was only going to be a temporary change. Maria arranged to move back to her mother's house and told me that she would be gone by the time I finished work the next day.

When I got back home the following day, I felt different. The flat was eerily quiet and I didn't like it. All of her clothes and personal belongings had been cleared out, and the place looked bare. It didn't look like a family home anymore, and I suddenly felt miserable and alone. The reality of my decision was beginning to sink in.

What on earth was I thinking? Had I made a big mistake? What if I had messed up big time?

I'd already been blown up by a bomb, lost my military career, my mother, my grandfather, and now I was adding my marriage to the

2005 and at my lowest point. My mother and grandfather had just passed away, and my military career was over as well as my marriage. I was drinking 4 litres of whisky a week to escape my troubles.

list. It was madness, utter madness. There were a lot of underlying issues and things to work out, but I still had hope in reconciliation.

Anything is possible, I thought. Deep down I didn't really want to end our marriage but I felt so bad about the way I was behaving, I was destroying her life as well as my own and I thought it was better to end it before things got really bad. She also had the support of her mother and family, a network I would now be without, and it was dawning on me that dealing with everything on my own was going to hurt, and it did.

I was already drinking every day, but now my stress levels were starting to go through the roof. My coping mechanism was to drink even more. Deep at the back of my mind, I thought at any minute Maria would walk through the door and say, "Come on then, let's sort this mess out." But it obviously wasn't going to happen. I left messages on her mobile and house phone asking her to contact me as I had things to say, but I got no response. I was spiralling into an emotional wreck. I didn't want to go to work, but I had no choice. Even when I was there, I couldn't think properly nor concentrate on the tasks at hand.

Five days after we separated, I got home and found a letter on the fireplace with some money. It was £60 from our joint bank account, Maria had withdrawn the balance and given it to me. I didn't care about the money, but the letter was different. I found it hard to read. It brought tears to my eyes and a lump firmly in my throat. It was a letter to say thank you for all the good times, along with the bad, that we had shared together and how sorry she was that it turned out this way. She also said how much of a struggle things had become for both of us, but no matter what happened, I would always have a special place in her heart.

I felt sick and empty. It suddenly registered with me that this was it, no going back. So I began to drink even more. I wasn't having whisky on my cornflakes or anything that extreme, but as soon as evening came, the bottle came out. Every night, I went through at least 10 double whiskies, and the minute the weekend came around, my alcohol consumption just intensified.

I would go through half a bottle of scotch before I'd even leave the flat, and once I got to The Nightingale, the local pub, I would start guzzling down pints.

In truth, the bomb blast may not have killed me, but if I wasn't careful, the resultant drinking might. Another big problem I had was that I wasn't eating properly. Some people, when they are stressed, might comfort eat, but I was the opposite. I couldn't face food, and the most I would get through was maybe 400 or 500 calories from Mars bars and microwaved junk food of some kind. Nothing substantial and certainly nothing of nutritional quality.

My bodyweight slowly began to drop, but I didn't consider the possible damage I was doing to myself. Mentally, I was falling into a dark place, and I needed help, but on the outside, people thought I was coping well. I was apparently doing a good job at covering the real effect all of this was having on me. My life was in absolute turmoil. One evening, I lost it. The large fish tank in the kitchen was playing up. The water heater had packed in and now the tropical fish were living in cold water. I was particularly drunk as I got on the phone to Maria to inform her that she needed to sort the fish out or they would die. She couldn't do anything at that time, and fuming, I slammed the phone down and turned around to punch the door. Unfortunately, in my drunken state, I missed the door completely and ended up punching the glass tank. My fist smashed straight through the glass, and 100 litres of water cascaded onto the kitchen floor. I could hear the young couple yelling in the flat below as the water seeped through the ceiling and into their kitchen. It didn't take long for the bloke to come running upstairs to find out what had happened.

I opened my door for him, and he stared at my kitchen, which was in a hell of a mess, with tropical fish flapping about on the saturated floor. What the hell could I do now? I'd drunk nearly a full bottle of whisky, so there was no way I could drive. I decided to fill the sink with warm water and hope the fish would survive. It didn't work, and a few hours later, they were dead.

One Saturday night, I ventured out alone into Cearleon and ended up in Bolero's. Feeling depressed as I sat alone smoking out the rear garden, I ended up chatting to an older lady. She asked what I was so miserable about, and for about 30 minutes, she sat and listened to me.

She could have walked away at any time, but she didn't. When I finished, she said, "Neil, you must write a book about this."

I replied, "Everyone has a story to tell, and why would anyone be interested in mine."

"Just write the book." She replied before leaving.

The following day, I thought about what that woman had said to me, but I didn't have a clue about how to write a book. Also, I didn't have any photos that could have been used in the book as the only images were inside my head. I never thought anymore about it.

I soon asked my father if I could stay with him for a while, and he agreed. I also decided that it was probably for the best if I gave up my flat as there were too many bad memories connected to it. Staying with my dad helped me to take my mind off some of my problems, but like me, he likes a drop of the old Scottish tipple, which could quickly become a problem.

I stayed with him for 3 weeks, sleeping on the floor, and every couple of days I'd go back to the flat to check my post and make sure no one had broken in. My flat was now totally empty. My father's mate ran a removal company, and he supplied me with some large cardboard boxes to pack up my stuff. I had it all sorted out within an hour.

My wooden bed was dismantled, together with the wardrobe, and the carpets were ripped up. To see it looking so bare was quite sobering. It was hard to imagine a young married couple lived there. It's the furniture and the company that makes the difference between a house and home and to have that difference so starkly emphasised was upsetting.

Every time I went out drinking, I seemed to get myself into trouble. I just attracted it. Leaving town one night worse for wear, I could see a large group of males and females in a circle. I wandered over to take a look. All of a sudden. People are pushed into each other. I fell backwards and into a girl who stood behind me. She ended up on the floor. As I turned around to help her up, a group of blokes were looking at me. They must have assumed that I hit her because I came under attack.

A number of punches landed on my head as I tried my best to get away. Eventually, they let me move on sore and bruised. I'd taken a bit of a kicking and hadn't done anything wrong other than being in the wrong place at the wrong time.

After 3 weeks with my father, I had second thoughts about the flat. Maybe I could stay there, decorate it, and try to make a fresh start. It was difficult moving back, and although I had been away for a few weeks, I still felt mentally insecure.

The evidence of this instability was evident on every door and most of the walls, which were peppered with holes from where I had lashed out in moments of uncontrollable anger. I didn't have the money to replace the doors, so a trip to B&Q for some filler was needed. I also got some cheap wallpaper, and my father got me a remnant of floor carpet for £100. It was starting to look more like a home again.

I was deeply depressed and unhappy. Yes, my flat was starting to look better, but the past still had a firm grip of me and wouldn't let go. I didn't have the motivation to do anything other than listen to music and drink whisky.

My bed was still in pieces as I couldn't even be bothered to reassemble it; instead, I chose to sleep on the mattress on the floor. I had curtains but no curtain rail as I had snapped it in half when I intended to move, so instead of buying another one, I used a satellite cable to hold them up. As for gas and electric, I had some, but they were constantly on emergency credit. I didn't have any lights either as the bulbs had blown, and I never replaced them, instead resorting to candles.

Looking back on that time, I can see that it was insane, and it nearly cost me my life.

On another Saturday evening out, I arranged to meet my father for a few drinks in Caerleon. I'd been doing a bit of painting earlier on and needed a bath before leaving. I filled the bath and hopped in, not noticing that I had knocked a bottle of white spirit that had been perched on the side, into the bath with me. Diluted or not, I can assure you that on the more sensitive regions, it hurt like hell. It felt like I had sprayed a bottle of deep heat over the area.

It was burning so badly that I had to sit in cold water for half an hour, and even when I finally got out, it took 2 hours for the pain to subside.

The rest of the night didn't improve either as my wallet was stolen, along with £50 and my driving licence. When I got home, I was very foolish, not to mention dangerous. With no functioning lights in my flat, I lit a candle and positioned it on top of a cardboard box. But as pissed as I was, I fell asleep not long after lighting it.

When I woke up the next morning I spent 5 minutes walking around before I noticed the candle was still burning, yes, burning on top of a cardboard box, and if that wasn't stupid enough I had even left the window open. It would only have taken a slight gust of wind to blow the candle over, and the whole place would have gone up in flames with me inside, unconscious after the hammering I'd given my liver.

Although I was still drinking a large amount, something happened to me mentally that forced me to cut down. My father kept telling me to watch my liver. I didn't have a clue what he meant. I was 25 years old and had never heard of alcohol liver disease. I didn't even know alcohol could kill. I just thought it gave you a bad head. Upon looking on-line, I came across a bloke in a hospital bed that was as yellow as a sunflower due to jaundice. Reading more into liver disease it triggered the start of my hypochondria.

I became convinced that I had developed liver disease from all the heavy drinking and found that I was regularly checking my skin and eyes to see if I had the yellow signs of jaundice. Every time I looked in the mirror, all I could see was a yellow person looking back at me. Of course, my skin and eyes were not yellow in reality. It was just my brain playing tricks on me. The human mind is so powerful that if you fixate so resolutely on something, in time, it becomes very real.

The fear of the damage I was doing quickly forced me to cut down my drinking and seek medical help for my possible liver damage. I went to see the doctor for an emergency appointment and waited 2 hours to be seen. There was no way I was waiting 6 weeks for an appointment. The 2-hour wait was bad enough.

The doctor asked me about my current psychological state and how much I was drinking. He gave me a piece of paper and told me to write down what I would typically drink during an ordinary week. The results were frightening.

I was advised that the "safe" limits were up to 28 units per week or about 14 pints.

When the doctor worked out my unit intake, it came to a massive 160 units, equivalent of about 70 pints a week. I agree that I was drinking a lot, but because I was drinking the units in whisky, it didn't seem that much to me.

The doctor said I'd need a liver function test to check if there was any damage and, if so, how bad it was. I knew this would send my anxiety through the roof as I'd have to wait a week for the results. For the next 7 days, I feared the worst. Terrible thoughts plagued me, but worst of all, I knew that if I was headed to an early grave, it was all my own doing. After 10 days, I couldn't wait any longer, I needed to know. I dialled the doctor's number and was given the results. I couldn't believe it. Amazingly, the tests came back, showing that my liver function was not quite what it should be, but that there was no real cause for concern.

Even though I now had my results, I wasn't convinced. After all, I was now a hypochondriac, and I could never be convinced. Maybe the tests were wrong, or maybe the doctor was lying. What if I was dying? I decided to wait a week and then go back for more tests. I didn't even make it that long.

I went straight back to see the doctor without the 7-day wait. The doctor tried his best to reassure me, explaining that they had completed 6 tests and only one had come back slightly raised. He advised me again to cut down on the alcohol and said I would be fine. He also gave me a prescription for the antidepressant medication Citalopram.

I was a shadow of my former self. It was coming up to 6 months since Maria and I had split up, and I was suffering from depression. My bodyweight was a shade over 10 stone, which, compared to my usual 13 stone, made me look skinny and weak. It's difficult to explain just how alone you feel and how the isolation creeps in. I was under constant criticism from family and friends, I guess they didn't really have any idea of what troubles I had actually faced, but it just added to my resentment.

As Christmas approached, I tried my best to get into the festive spirit. I propped a tree in the corner, and because my liver results were fine, I started to drink again. My fridge was bare with the exception of a few cans of lager. I also had a couple of bottles of whisky and some Irish Meadow, which was a cut price Baileys substitute. I honestly expected Maria to drop a Christmas card through the door, but nothing came.

It turned out to be the worst Christmas day I've ever had. I ate dinner at my sister's before going back to my grandmother's with my father for a couple of drinks. It was that bad that by 6 pm, I was on the sofa bed, ready to sleep. Time rolled on, and by mid-January, I felt that on the whole, my life was shit and was going to forever remain that way.

Chapter 12

It's that idiot Selina

DURING ONE OF my regular nights out in the city, I met a girl. Why she wanted to talk to me, though, God only knows. I was skinny, weighed 10 stone soaking wet, and had more than a couple of screws loose.

I caught sight of her sitting outside in the pub garden with her friends, so I walked over and started chatting to her. I can't remember what I said, if it was good or bad, but her friends stayed with her. I couldn't have been that charismatic as I ended up going home alone.

Two weeks later, after a night out drinking a lot more than I care to think about, I staggered towards the taxi rank for a ride home. While I was waiting, I bumped into the same girl from 2 weeks before, again out with her friends. One of her friends recognised me, and I heard her whisper, "Look over there, it's that idiot, Selina. The one you were talking to the other week."

Idiot, well that's a first. The girl came over to me and we talked for about 15 minutes, this time I managed to get her name, Selina.

Just before she jumped into a taxi, I asked her if we could meet up again. She said yes and handed me her phone number.

I gave her a ring the next day and asked if she fancied meeting up. She agreed and said to meet her after work on Monday afternoon, at the time she worked for BT in customer services.

I was parked up outside McDonalds on the high street when

Selina came to meet me. We went to a pub just outside Bettws and spent a bit of time getting to know each other. I also wanted to show her my flat, not that it was a palace, but it was my own place. She was hesitant at first but then agreed as long as I dropped her back home later in the evening.

I don't think she was impressed with the flat. In all honesty, it was a shithole. I didn't even have a proper bed put together. My satellite cable was still holding the curtains up, and I didn't even have a sofa to sit on – I was using a green council recycling box when I wasn't sitting on the floor.

Selina lived with her parents in St Brides, which was on the other side of Newport. She had not long come out of a long-term relationship herself and had moved back home until she got back on her feet. It seemed we had something in common there. As promised, I dropped her back home that night.

I personally wasn't keen on jumping straight into another relationship, especially after the last one had almost driven me to the point of suicide. For all my reservations, though, I couldn't deny that it was nice to have company.

Over the next few weeks, Selina started to treat the flat as her own. She would come home from work with curtain rails, picture frames, and other little bits to tidy the place up. It felt like life was starting to pick up again.

She left BT and started working in the evening at her family's fish bar in Magor, while I began working for a friend who was a butcher. I was their delivery driver and would spend 7 hours a day dropping off meat to pubs and nursing homes within a 60-mile radius.

Now that Selina was living with me, the amount I was drinking dropped dramatically. I even quit smoking and started to do a bit of running around the estate.

One day, Selina went and did a full weeks' food shop in Asda. The cupboards, fridge, and freezer were full for the first time in ages. I loved it. There was so much choice. When I lived alone, I hardly ever ate anything, and even when I did, it was whatever I could get from the local spar. Things were definitely looking up.

After we'd been together for a year, we decided to get a dog. Selina wanted some tiny ankle biter, but I wanted a German Shepherd, a breed I loved, having grown up with them.

After much debate, Selina let me have my way, German Shepherd it was. We began by looking through the free ads and, after a few weeks, found a promising advert. There was a mixture of six dogs; 4 males and 2 bitches. They were 10 weeks old from a KC registered breeder based in Bettws, Bridgend.

We had a limited window of time to get to the breeder and see the dogs, but we were really keen to put down a deposit. I suppose we could've waited, but I was anxious not to miss this opportunity as puppies are often snapped up within hours.

Selina was adamant that there was no way we could make it to the dogs and get her back home in time for work. However, I'd recently gotten myself an E36 M3 Evolution and reassured her, with a grin, that there was plenty of time. The breeder agreed to meet us at McArthur Glen Designer Outlet, and when we arrived, I instantly fell in love with the dog. We brought a puppy home with us and now had a family pet named Tara.

Having a dog really helped to balance out and stabilise my mood swings and depression. I can appreciate now why dogs are sometimes used to help those suffering from PTSD. While the dog made me feel relaxed, she also liked to cause trouble in the flat as she chewed through pretty much everything that Selina owned; expensive handbags, watches, the lot.

I soon lost my job as a delivery driver and was back to scraping money together wherever I could. I took the initiative to register myself as self-employed and started doing odd jobs alongside my father, small jobs like car seat repairs and fitting convertible hoods to cars. Meanwhile, Selina was now out of the fish bar and working for a large company in Cwmbran.

We plodded on for the next 9 months, making ends meet, until one day Selina told me she might be pregnant. A shop bought pregnancy test quickly confirmed her suspicions. I was both excited and worried by the thought of having a baby, but I was definitely more worried.

We were living in a small flat with a big dog, and I didn't even have a decent income behind me. When we went for an ultrasound scan, it became all the more overwhelming. We were expecting twins. It was a massive shock, and neither of us knew what to make of the news.

Thankfully, we had some help from Selina's family with things like buying a cot and a car seat, but it was still rather costly.

While I was tremendously happy about these little baby boys coming along, I was nonetheless worried about where we were going to live. The flat wasn't at all ideal. Even with just myself, Selina, and the dog living there, you could hardly swing a cat. With two added people, it would be impossible.

It wasn't just down to the space. It was Tara. I couldn't risk having a large dog and newborns in the same space. Potentially, all it would take was for her to move, and the damage could be devastating. Despite this, though, I didn't want to rehome Tara either.

Selina's mother owned a property in Newport and told us that once the tenants moved out, we could move in. It was a 2-bedroom newbuild house in the Celtic Horizons part of Newport. The rent was almost twice as much as the flat, but in return, we acquired more than twice the space, including a back garden and a garage. It would be enormous in comparison to the flat.

I was looking forward to moving in, although I can't say I wasn't anxious at the prospect of giving up the security of my own place, even though we'd been together for 3 years and were having children.

I had first-hand experience over and over again that life can change for better or worse in the blink of an eye. If it did change for the worse, I would most likely end up on my arse living on the streets. I couldn't help but fall back into negative thinking as I'd had such a rough time in recent years.

As part of the moving process, I built a kennel for Tara because she would have to sleep in the garden. I bought a 6-foot garden shed from B&Q and knocked 3 feet off of it. I padded the whole thing out with foam and then carpeted the bottom. It looked really good and was well insulated and dry.

When it was time to move our possessions in, we booked the dog into kennels. There was plenty to shift, and with Selina 8 months pregnant, I was moving most of the heavy stuff on my own. Two days later, I handed the keys to the flat back to the council. I was dreading their inspection and repair bills.

Three doors had to be replaced, as well as fixing four large holes in the plasterboard walls. They were also likely to charge me for items I couldn't take with me. There was an old sofa we had bought, as well as a big wardrobe. I only had the use of a small van and couldn't fit them in. I can't remember how much the bill came to, but I do remember having to set up a payment plan to clear the balance.

Once we had moved our stuff in, it was time for me to collect the dog and bring her home, i then set about decorating the place, the living room first, followed by my future boys' nursery.

Although we were now in our new home, we didn't want visitors, mostly due to not actually owning a sofa. We had a 32" flat screen TV on the wall, but all we had to sit on was a small beanbag. That was it. We managed to rectify that just before the boys were due and got hold of a nice sofa from Next clearance. At least we now had something decent to sit on.

Selina was soon in hospital, and the twins were finally on their way. The pregnancy had been a rough 9 months for us, more so for Selina. For at least half of her last trimester, Selina was an in-patient in hospital due to various problems caused by the deadly pre-eclampsia, a condition which gave her swollen legs and prompted her blood pressure to shoot up.

After a long 11 hours in labour, Selina finally gave birth to our 2 boys; Nico and Fabio. It was without doubt the happiest day of my life and one I would remember forever.

Despite everything that had happened to me, I had a lot to be grateful for. Not only did the birth of my boys make me feel like I had been re-born myself, but they gave me a reason to live again. I was determined to set a good example for them so that one day, they would look up to me for support and guidance. I also had Selina to thank. If I hadn't met her, who knows where I'd be now.

Probably dead given the lifestyle I was living at the time.

Shortly after the twins were born, we received worrying news. Doctors had detected a problem with Fabio's heart, and more tests were needed to find out the problem.

With Fabio's condition now on our minds, we weren't able to enjoy our time at home as a family until the root cause had been identified. Selina remained in hospital, I was at home, and the dog was back in the kennels.

We had decided to keep the dog there for a few days while Selina and the babies could settle in at home without the added strain of keeping a close eye on Tara. I was only allowed to visit the hospital during visiting hours, but I always tried to stay a bit longer than they allowed so I could spend more time with Selina.

A few days had passed since the twins' birth, and I was alone at home watching TV when there was a knock at the door. It was my grandmother; she had come to congratulate us. She also said that she'd spoken to my father, and they had both decided that I would get rid of the dog. I had already considered rehoming Tara myself, but if I did, it would be my choice, no one else's.

I was well aware of the dangers of having a large dog around young children. After all, I had been bitten on the face as a child by a German Shepherd. Although it was just an accident, I knew how easily it could happen.

However, I am a very loyal person not just to other people but in every aspect of my life, be it a pet or a job. Hence why I had built the kennel and made it as warm and comfortable as possible.

Another thing that irritated me was the number of my family members who thought I was weak because I was upset about giving up my dog. I wonder if they would be so keen to give up their pets, I doubt it!

I knew that I had to re-home Tara because it wasn't safe to keep her in the house with newborns, but it wasn't fair to make her live in the garden 24/7 either. It was a decent sized garden covered with grass, but where she'd been running around, the grass had become chewed up, and after a week, it looked more like a muddy pigsty.

Regardless of coming to this decision myself, it didn't make it any easier when the time came to let her go.

A friend of Selina's mother had shown an interest in the dog, so I offered Tara to her. She accepted, and we arranged to meet at the kennels the following day so that the dog could be collected and begin her new life.

The next day was truly heartbreaking. A dog might only be an animal to some people, but she was my dog, and I had raised her from a puppy. I hated the fact that I had to give her away to someone else.

Selina's mother's friend, Jackie, was waiting with me at the kennels while the kennel worker went to fetch Tara. I hadn't seen her in 4 days, but as soon as she saw me, she came running over, jumping up on me and trying to lick me in that unconditional loving manner dogs possess.

It was a horrible feeling to just pass her over to a stranger like that. She wouldn't have understood what was going on either, and I felt like I'd let her down. She had been a loyal and faithful dog, yet here I was giving her away. It wasn't a decision I had taken lightly.

The next day, it was time for Selina and the babies to come home from the hospital. It's funny, we'd been preparing for this day for so long, yet now that they were here, we didn't know what to do with them. There was no "good parent" guide for you to follow. It's just one steep learning curve.

All they did was eat, sleep, and then repeated the cycle over and over. Night-time feeds were also very taxing as there were two of them, so we couldn't take it in turns. Every 2 hours, we both got up to feed them. It was exhausting.

A week later, we had an appointment to see the heart specialist about Fabio. After a comprehensive examination, it turned out to be a murmur. It would need to be monitored over the next couple of years, but with any luck he'd grow out of it once he was a bit older and more developed.

Technically, I was still self-employed, but the income just wasn't enough. Even with my Army pension, we were really struggling. I didn't want this, I wanted better for my kids. I would have to start looking for another job to give them the life I wanted for them.

Chapter 13

Cabin fever

I STARTED TO look for jobs right away. It had to be something with good hours and guaranteed work. Being ex-military, I thought that a role as a security officer might suit me, as every ex-serviceman I knew seemed to be working in that field. I knew the wage wasn't going to be great, but I also knew that I'd probably get the opportunity to do extra hours, which would help make up the difference.

I didn't have any savings, so I couldn't afford to pay for the course to get my SIA licence. The licence was compulsory, and I'd have to apply to the Security Industry Authority if I wanted to work in that type of business.

It was by chance that the Job Centre was offering to fund a course for people who were registered as unemployed to enable them to get back into paid work. I went along to one of their job clubs and was delighted when they told me they would fund the training costs for my SIA licence.

The next course wasn't due to start for another month, but when it finally began, I found that it was much easier than I'd anticipated. It was only a week long with two written tests and a physical intervention test to finish. I'd have to be as thick as shit to fail.

All that followed was a simple CRB check, and 4 weeks later, my new SIA licence arrived in the post.

I looked for work and didn't care too much about the location, hours, or pay. At that point, any job would do. A position became available working as a Port Security Officer at Cardiff docks. I applied straight away and was asked to attend an interview at the company's office in Bridgend.

Given the fact that I was polite, well turned out, and held an exemplary military record, I was offered the job there and then. The pay was only minimum wage, but they were offering 60 hours a week, so I could live with that.

When I turned up on my first day, the team supervisor issued me with a uniform before giving me a tour of the docks and the facilities. I was then led to the cabin that I'd be working in.

The cabin was very small, measuring around 16 feet by 8 feet, and the inside was sparse. There were a couple of amenities like a kettle, microwave, toilet, radio, plus a computer screen linked to the Automatic Number Plate Recognition ("ANPR") system, and that was it. I then learned that I'd be working here on my own. I'm alone in this minuscule cabin for 60 hours a week!

Two hours into my debut shift, the senior port security officer came in to meet me. He was a short, friendly chap in his early 50's and had previously held a senior rank in the Royal Marines with over 20 years' service.

He knew that I had been injured by a bomb blast and that I had a few stress related issues, but he didn't know quite how badly these problems affected me. He presumed I might struggle with the job and although I assured him that I'd be fine, he told me that if I had any issues, not to hesitate, I was to go and see him. Maybe he could read my mind.

The first month passed by without any teething problems, and I was settling in nicely, content to be learning on the job.

However, I soon began to feel restless and would spend ages clock watching. It was a long day sitting in that tiny box alone. The job itself was easy enough, just lifting and closing a barrier. Even a child could do it, but over the next few weeks, my mental state started to decline. I was listening to the radio one day when it was mentioned that during a person's lifetime, their ears and nose never stopped growing.

Well, I didn't believe this, so I googled it, and I wish I hadn't. The results took me to a disorder called rhinophyma. This horrible condition that usually affects those who suffer from rosacea. It affects the nose and causes it to grow bulbous, red, and lumpy, like a bunch of purple grapes. I couldn't get the image out of my head, and what was worse, over time I began to think I was developing the condition. I was driving myself crazy thinking about it. Every time I looked in the mirror, I could see my nose riddled with this ailment.

What the hell was happening to me? I had no idea. I think the isolation did funny things to me – I literally had cabin fever. Over the years, scientists have carried out research on monkeys kept in solitary confinement, and it's no surprise that the consequences are never good. Even though my security cabin had two windows, I was still suffering from extreme anxiety and in combination with the hyperactive lifestyle I was leading, the effect on my mind was similar to that of a prisoner in solitary confinement.

As well as worrying about the rhinophyma, I was convinced my hair was falling out, and this added to my already sky-high anxiety. I would rub my head over the sink and count how many hairs were in there. I would then Google to find out the average number of hairs we lose. It got to the point where I had to remove the mirror and all the other triggers.

Many nights at home I'd find myself crying alone from what this job was doing to me. I hated it, but with bills coming through, I had no choice but to keep putting myself through this mental ordeal, day after day.

I couldn't talk to anyone about how I felt, not even my wife. No one would understand how the job was affecting me so much. I no longer had a social life. The hours I worked meant I only got the chance to see my children on weekends as they were fast asleep in bed by the time I came home at night.

Something had to give, and luckily, it did. An advert came on the radio for the upcoming Cardiff Half Marathon in October. In a snap decision, I thought, "sod it, I'm doing this."

I was no longer as fit as I once was, but that didn't stop me. I got my mobile phone out and signed up straight away. I thought I would make it a bit more interesting and speed march the course whilst carrying a 40lb military rucksack and raise some money for Help4Heroes.

I announced my challenge on Facebook and set up a donation page. No more than 10 minutes later, I received a message from John Williams. My platoon sergeant during my infantry training at Catterick. He was still serving, now a colour sergeant and a qualified fitness instructor. He asked for my phone number and said he would like to take part as well. He called me a few minutes later to go through some training plans, and we arranged to meet up in a few weeks time for a training session in the Brecon Beacons.

With this future challenge ahead of me, I gained a new sense of purpose. It was something to take my mind off the mental torture of the security cabin. I managed to get hold of a military rucksack from a friend and started training at once. I even forked out £150 for a new pair of Lowa combat boots. They were pricey, but over time, they had proved themselves to be one of the best boots money could buy.

So, every morning at 02:30, I bounded out of bed, gulped down a quick cup of coffee, and was out the door by 03:00 with my rucksack strapped firmly to my back. There was an 8-mile route around my neighbourhood that I completed in 2 hours. Once I got back, I had just enough time for a hurried shower before leaving for my 12-hour shift at work. It was really exhausting, but it was the only way I could train, work, and still have time to see Selina in the evenings.

While I was at work, I was still suffering from my mental health issues, so I kept trying to focus on the half marathon to keep my mind busy. I needed to flood my mind with positivity to keep the negative thoughts at bay. Early one Saturday morning, I arranged to meet John at the Storey Arms in Brecon.

The Storey Arms is a former mountain rescue station turned outdoor activity centre, around 8 miles north of Merthyr Tydfil

Fitness training on the Brecon beacons.

on the A470. With a large car park opposite, it serves as the main starting point for those attempting to climb the highest mountain in the Brecon Beacons, Pen Y Fan.

I was feeling reasonably fit as I loaded up my 60-lb rucksack in preparation for our ascent. John turned up with a little day sack, and I found myself wondering where his real rucksack was. Less than 10 minutes into the first climb, I was massively regretting taking so much weight. I was knackered and couldn't catch my breath, yet John was having no issue with his petite little day sack, trotting past while smiling at me. The 60lb had felt alright in the car park, but it was a different story once we were on the hills.

We ended up covering around 10 miles. A bit of a lung buster, but a good day out. The next time we would see each other would be in Cardiff on the day of the race.

Every day, I carried on training alone and made good use of the Brecon and Monmouthshire canal, which was only a 10-minute drive from my house. In work, I had a big collection bucket and couldn't believe the amount that had been raised so far. With this newfound energy, 8 weeks flew by, and before I knew it, race day had arrived. My cousin had also served in the military and was doing the run using a rucksack as well, albeit it with less weight.

It had been years since I had done a speed march of this distance, but I couldn't wait to start. It was hard work, but I finished in a fraction over 3 hours. I wasn't sure what time John had finished, but he was halfway back to Bridgend by the time I crossed the line.

It wasn't about competing with John, nor was it about the overall time I finished in. It was all about the challenge and completing it while fundraising for charity at the same time. The day after the half marathon, I went into work with blistered feet and handed in my notice. Without a doubt, working alone in that cabin had a damaging effect on me. I snapped my SIA licence in half and vowed never to return to that kind of job again.

Chapter 14

The Taff Trail

WITH THE CARDIFF Half Marathon finished, I felt a great sense of personal achievement, and when I counted up the money I had raised, it felt all the more worthwhile. The donations came to around £1300 which was a decent amount of money for a 13 mile run and would be put to good use by Help4Heroes.

A few weeks later, I received the divorce notification from Maria. I always told myself I would never put myself through another marriage after the stress of the last one. With Selina, though, things felt different. We had already been together for 5 years by this point, and with 2 young children, it felt almost inevitable.

A few months of saving for a ring, and it was time to propose. Her answer was yes! We started planning the wedding practically straight away. Almost all the venues we visited were out of our price range, which was disheartening. However, Selina's family saved the day when they told us they'd booked the Celtic Manor Resort for our big day.

We couldn't believe it. The Celtic Manor was incredible, and there was no way myself or Selina could have saved up for that venue ourselves.

My father offered to pay for the honeymoon, an all-inclusive Egyptian resort for a week. The wedding was beginning to take shape, the only downside being that I had to wear a suit. After wearing my smart military parade uniform the first time around, I now felt somewhat underdressed.

With everything in its place, we had a stag do and hen party to enjoy. I ventured into Caerleon along with my father and uncle while Selina and the girls headed to Swansea and Wine Street.

The big day was amazing, Selina looked beautiful in her dress. The weather couldn't have been any better, and the Celtic Manor was worth every penny. We ate some outstanding food in the Terry M restaurant, and then some more delicious food at the evening party. It was definitely a night to remember for a long time. We even ended up in the presidential suite, courtesy of the resort.

Two days after saying our vows, we travelled to Egypt. We were staying at the Tropitel Sahl Hasheesh, which was by Hurghada. The place was amazing, except for the first night when Selina's forehead ballooned to double the size after being attacked by some sort of bug. Thankfully, the swelling diminished overnight, and we were free to make the most of our honeymoon.

Not long after getting home, I began to look for another challenge I could do, one that was longer and tougher. I wanted to push myself to the limit. After a few cold ones, a thought popped into my head from my military days. More specifically, from a time from when I intended to do the SAS selection course. Back then, I was fit and determined, but even then, I knew that candidates were made to walk more than 40 miles carrying a heavy rucksack, and it seemed like a superhuman feat of endurance. It was something I wasn't entirely sure I was physically capable of doing.

Even though I was pretty fit now, mentally, I wasn't as strong as I was back then. Added to that, I would be training with an impaired knee. In the face of this, I was determined to attempt a long-distance solo walk.

I was considering what suitable walks I could do when my buddy Mark, who I grew up with, suggested the Taff Trail. I'd never heard of it, but a quick google search quickly brought me up to speed. The Taff Trail is an extensive walking and cycling route that stretches for 55 miles between the market town of Brecon and Cardiff Bay. It was perfect.

It was a simple plan; I would walk the whole way while carrying a 40-lb rucksack, aiming to finish in 18 hours. I wanted to find a worthy charity and came across Scotty's Little Soldiers.

The charity was formed a few years earlier by a lady who had lost her husband, Scott, whilst he was serving in Afghanistan. The charity organised day trips and the like for children who have lost a parent serving in the Armed Forces. For me, this was certainly worthy of some support.

I picked a date, Friday 23rd August, and planned to start in Brecon at 03:00. I solidly hit the gym every day to build up my stamina, adding in weight training to gain strength, which would assist with both the walking and carrying the weight.

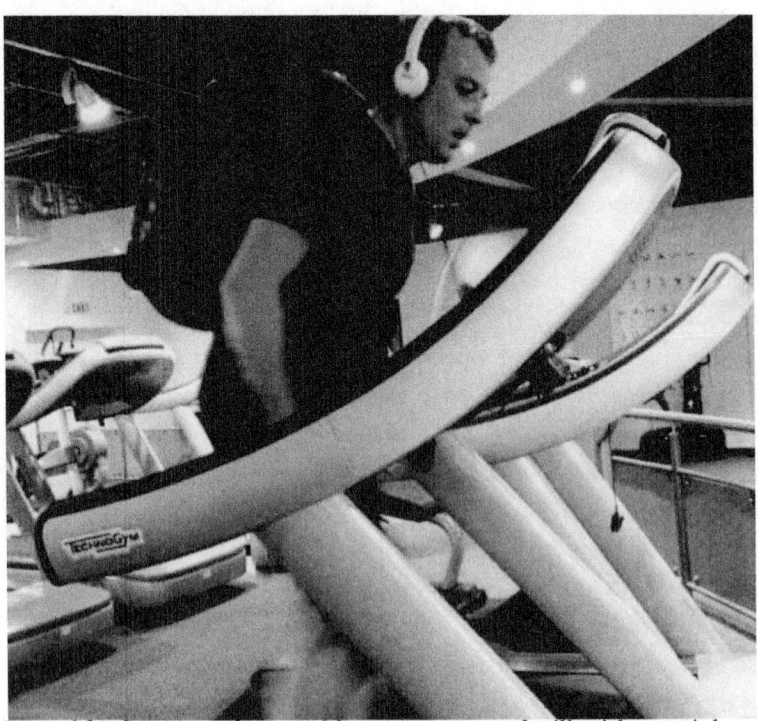

I would often spend several hours on a treadmill with a weighted rucksack just building physical and mental endurance.

Despite all of the effort I was putting in, I was still unsure whether I was physically capable of walking such a distance with that amount of weight in the time limit I'd set myself. Even in the military, 10 years before, the most I had covered was about 20 miles, and that was as part of a team.

In the Army, I found there was very little requirement for self motivation as the training staff would provide more than enough. On this occasion, I would be covering almost three times the distance and without any of the support.

A couple of weeks before the event, a friend recommended that I cycle the route first to familiarise myself and get a feel for what I was up against. It made sense, but I was concerned that it might turn out to be more arduous than I had imagined and make me doubt my ability to succeed. I decided against it, reasoning that I was fit and determined, and no matter what obstacle I came up against, I would just hit it hard and crack on.

A week before the walk, Dave, my uncle, said he wanted to take part. Instead of going along the entire Taff Trail, he would walk the 35-mile route from Brecon to his home in Cwmbran using the canal route. We'd start at the same place, the Brecon Theatre, then walk together for 2 miles until we split to go ahead on our chosen paths.

The day of the walk arrived and sadly I had to go to work first, but the minute I got home I packed my rucksack with all my gear; plenty of food, first aid kit, head torch and batteries, map, spare socks and blister plasters, plus the crucial stuff like warm clothing, waterproofs, and a mobile phone. I also chucked in a pair of trainers, just in case.

For fluid, I would carry 8 litres, 6 of which would be water and 2 litres of Lucozade divided between two CamelBak water bladders. I also carried a huge flag emblazoned with the charity's name strapped to my rucksack. I never did bother to weigh my pack, but it felt heavier than 40lb. After all, I was carrying 18lb of fluid before counting any of the other kit.

As we intended to set off at 03:00 I would have to get up at 00:30. An early night was on the cards, not that I got one. I went to the local chippy at 19:00 to grab a pie and chips and was hoping to be asleep by 20:00.

I was lying in bed when Selina put the TV on and switched over to the Big Brother launch event. Damn. I knew I'd have no chance now. I was tossing and turning and couldn't switch off. I was so restless. I desperately needed some sleep, but I was so psyched I couldn't relax.

I went to sleep on the sofa as a last-ditch attempt for some shut eye. It was pitch black downstairs, and I even tried counting sheep, but nothing worked. It was now 23:30, only 1 hour before I had to get up.

I did eventually drift off as I awoke to my alarm sounding, feeling infinitely worse for the small amount of sleep I'd managed to get. I would have fallen straight back to sleep had I not had this walk ahead of me.

I sat on the sofa with a cup of strong coffee and a thousand-yard stare affixed to my face. I started wrapping zinc oxide tape to my feet, all the while thinking of the task that lay ahead.

I was looking forward to it but didn't feel as confident now as I was so bloody tired. I'd only had around 45 minutes of sleep since 06:00 the previous morning, and the next kip I'd get would be when I finished the walk. If I finished, that is.

My father took Dave and me to Brecon and Bang on 03:00 we set off from the theatre. For the first 2 miles, we followed the canal together, with my flag catching on every low bridge I passed under. We soon got to the point where we'd agreed to split off and go our separate ways; Dave continued to Cwmbran via Abergavenny, whilst I followed the trail to Cardiff Bay. I would be passing through a number of towns, including Merthyr and Pontypridd, but first, I had the mountains of the Brecon Beacons to negotiate.

The first 8 miles took me through some small villages before I ended up at Talybont Reservoir and the beginning of the Beacons. The next 5 miles were a real leg and lung buster as the trail climbed all the way up to its highest point, Torpantau. I was doing well for time, I had covered the first 13 miles in 4 hours and was doing well. It was pretty much all downhill from here, but still about 40 miles no less.

I trekked through Pontsticill Reservoir and the town of Merthyr, but by now, my legs were aching, and my feet were starting to hurt. I allowed myself a quick 5-minute break to carry out some running repairs. I had a few blisters beginning to form, so I popped them and slapped some more tape over the top. Fresh socks now on, and the tougher terrain behind me, I decided to swap my heavy boots for my "go faster" trainers.

The next part of the trail took me along a path that runs past the little village of Aberfan, the scene of the terrible landslide in the 1960's that sadly claimed over a hundred young children's lives when it destroyed their school. I could see the memorial garden as I passed by.

With a bit of running, I soon made it to Pontypridd. I was feeling confident that I might just do this. I had about 20 miles to go, what's 20 miles? But I may have spoken too soon. As I reached the roundabout by the university, the weather took a turn for the worse, and my feet got soaked. Typically, I also managed to get lost. I carried on into a housing estate and lost the trail. I didn't have the foggiest idea where to go and there was no one to ask for help.

Things had been going so well for me, and it looked as though I may end up failing on the home straight. Thankfully, my luck changed, and some local kids took pity on me as they spent 10 minutes guiding me back to the trail. It was a massive relief when I finally caught sight of the sign for the Taff Trail again, so much so that I got out a packet of sweets to celebrate. I was back on track.

I went past Castle Coch and was soon on the outskirts of Cardiff. This was it. I only had a few miles left. There was no way I could fail now. My father phoned me for an update and told me that Dave had done well but had ultimately jacked it in at Goytre Wharf, about 10 miles short. He had still managed 25 miles, which was pretty good going, considering he didn't train for it. I told my father I was near the castle roughly 2 miles away and to give me half an hour and I'd be there.

As I neared Techniquest I could see my father waiting for me. I had this sense of pride in finishing it, but mostly because it was over.

I'd gotten less than an hour's worth of kip in the last 40 hours and had walked over 50 miles alone carrying a weighted rucksack, all within 16 hours. I was physically exhausted. Never in my life had I felt so fatigued. During the 20-minute drive back to Newport, my legs started to cramp up and I could barely walk.

As soon as I got home, I necked a bottle of Newcastle Brown Ale before jumping in the shower. Bloody hell, was I sore! My shoulders and back had been rubbed raw from the rucksack, I had nasty groin chafing, and my feet were red and puckered with blisters. The second I got out of the shower, I collapsed in a heap on the bed.

Selina woke me up a couple of hours later when she got home, with a large chips and Doner kebab for me – what a wife! I needed to preserve my energy because the next day I was off on my neighbour Mark's stag do. Although I was massively proud of myself for walking such a distance, I swore afterwards that I'd never walk the Taff Trail again.

The next challenge I set myself was going to be on a treadmill. I was already a member of DW Fitness in Newport, so what better place to stage my challenge. I spoke to the manager about the possibility of doing a non-stop run/walk over 15 hours carrying a 30lb rucksack. She thought I was mad but agreed that I could do it there. I decided that I would raise funds for Help4Heroes again.

A friend of mine from my military days, Lee asked if he could take part. He wanted to raise funds for the Royal Gwent Hospital, Special Care Baby Unit. I was more than happy to let him take part, and we decided on Thursday 14th November as the date for our challenge.

While I was training, I planned to have another go at the Cardiff Half Marathon in October, a month before my treadmill endeavour. I was now much fitter than I was in the previous year, so this would be interesting.

The weight of my rucksack was going to be even heavier this time at 52 lb, but I also swapped my boots for trainers. I parked at the Bluebirds Stadium, so there was a 2 mile walk just to get to the start line outside Cardiff Castle. I had a large burger to fuel myself up, then shorty afterwards I was packed like a sardine in a can with thousands of others awaiting the final countdown. Normally I would start of with some fast walking to warm up before jogging, but as I had so many people around me I had to jog from the start. I covered the first 3 miles in about 25 minutes and was feeling great.

At around the 9 mile point, I could see a team of Royal Marines a distance behind me who were also carrying weighted Bergen's, so they became my extra motivation. I gave everything I could to make sure they didn't catch up to me and they didn't. My rigorous training over the past 12 months had paid off, and I crossed the finish line in 2 hours and 12 minutes. A respectable time for a normal runner, but as I was loaded with the equivalent of a small child on my back, my time was brilliant. I was almost one whole hour quicker than the previous year.

Every day, I trained hard at the gym, with long periods spent on the treadmill building up a solid endurance capacity. Three hour sessions became part of my normal routine, but even that didn't prepare me mentally for what 15 plus hours would be like.

The day before the challenge, my son developed a bad cough. There was no way I could carry out the challenge with the same symptoms he had, so I wore a 3M mask to avoid catching any germs from him. The morning of the challenge arrived, and Lee and I were raring to go.

Most of my treadmill sessions had been between 2 and 3 hours long, but just a few hours into the challenge, you could see that Lee was struggling. From then on, it only got worse. The gym became really quiet, but the few that were there chatted to us every now and again. It was still going to be a long and boring day. It would be around 4 in the afternoon before it would start to get busy, but by 2 in afternoon Lee had nothing left in the tank. Despite this, he had still covered 28 miles with very little training, which is an amazing achievement.

For the remainder of the challenge, he supported me with motivation and cold drinks while walking slowly on the machine beside me. I finally finished the walk at 22:00, having covered a shade over 52 miles, or the equivalent of two marathons. I wasn't as exhausted as the Taff Trail walk but my feet were in bits.

Unlike outside, where you get a mixture of terrain and the chance to vary your foot position, the treadmill belt continually wears into the same parts of your feet. When I got home, I jumped into the shower and felt immense pain as the water trickled over all of the sores I'd developed. I had to recover quickly though, because on Monday, I was starting my Gym Instructor Course in Cardiff.

I was really excited about starting the course. I was super fit, and thanks to the endurance challenges I had already accomplished, I felt like I was in a position where I could help motivate and inspire others to achieve the same standards.

Although I had declared never to take on the Taff Trail again, in February, I planned to repeat the challenge. I guess you could put it down to the same feeling you get when you wake up with a hangover. Everyone claims that they'll never drink again, but that usually only lasts until the following weekend.

The charity I had chosen to support this time was for a young child from Newport called Casey Hard. The charity was called Casey's Cause and helped to pay for specialist equipment. Casey, a little boy aged 2 years old, suffered from severe epilepsy, cerebral palsy and spastic quadriplegia following a traumatic birth at the Royal Gwent Hospital.

As if this wasn't bad enough for the family, Casey's father Anthony, a corporal in the RAF, was recovering from brain cancer surgery. It seemed a natural fit to support them.

As the challenge approached, an old school friend of mine, Jamie Boycott, got in touch to tell me that he'd like to do the charity walk with me. I had no issue with this, and after walking the trail solo the first time around, I knew it would be nice to have some company for the long slog ahead.

I went to visit Casey and his father at their home a month before the walk to collect some charity collection pots. I also contacted the local newspaper to drum up extra support for the challenge, as well as getting fancy t-shirts printed too.

As part of our training, Jamie and I went for a mountain trek over the Beacons. It was bitterly cold with a decent amount of snowfall as we made our way towards Pen Y Fan. All was fine on the way up. However, coming back down was a scary experience as we got caught in a severe snowstorm just below Corn Du. Unable to keep our eyes open, we had completely lost the footpath.

"Neil mate, where's the path?" I heard Jamie call out.

"Just keep heading down," I shouted back.

Five minutes later, the weather completely changed. The sky was clear, and the sun was shining, it's amazing how the weather in the Beacons could change in minutes.

The day of our challenge arrived, and without going into too much detail, it was a complete nightmare. First of all, while walking through the forest, we came up against a 12ft no access barrier blocking our path.

Apparently there were tree cutting operations taking place, but we reasoned that at 02:00 we'd probably be safe, so we made our way through the barrier as the only other choice was an 8 mile round trip along the other side of the reservoir. Sod that.

Later on, we encountered numerous hindrances, like me dropping my brand new HTC mobile on the ground, smashing it to pieces, and to top it all off, we ended up being locked inside Sophia Gardens, and spent ages trying to find a way out. Eventually we did and reasoned that we had already covered around 55 miles, possibly more, including the diversions, and raised a few hundred pounds to help support young Casey, so that was enough for the day.

Wales were playing at millennium stadium that evening and Cardiff was packed. I grabbed a can of Guinness from my rucksack as a sort of celebration drink and almost instantly felt tipsy due to my tiredness. Myself and Jamie looked worse for wear outside the castle when Wales rugby legend Robert Jones came to ask what our walk was about. He had a photo with us and said, you're both legends for doing that. We are not legends but it was nice of him to say it.

Chapter 15

Sod your council tax

I WAS STILL working alongside my father, trimming out the cars, but we were clashing all the time. We both had different ways of doing things, with different attitudes to life. Tensions were rising, and I remember on one particular day, I'd had enough. I slammed my tools down and stormed out. I couldn't take it anymore. On the face of it, it was a stupid idea as I needed all the money I could get, I was already behind with all of my utility bills. However, I felt certain that I would find another job within a week or so, I was a hard worker and had a good CV.

Selina wasn't pleased in the least, but she understood and said that no matter what happened, we would get through it together. I started my job hunt by sending my CV to every available job on Indeed.com. I must have sent at least 10 CV's a day but got no responses. I even tried phoning companies directly, but still no joy.

I was starting to worry now. The MOT on my car was due to expire, and I was slowly getting unfriendly bills through the post. I was in a bad situation that would only get worse if I didn't do something fast. I had no choice but to cancel all my direct debits as they were being paid out but kept getting returned, which in turn meant I was being hit with extra charges on my bank account. It was a vicious circle and I didn't know what to do. My car was the first priority as I needed to get the kids to school. Plus, when I did find a job, I would need to be willing to travel. I booked the car in for a test and just hoped and prayed it would pass. I only had £150 to last me until I found a new job. The car didn't pass the MOT, so on top of the £40 test fee, I was looking at a repair bill of at least £450. What the hell was I going to do.

I couldn't take out a loan as I had a poor credit score, and I wouldn't be granted an overdraft on my bank account either. Over the next few weeks, even more bills came through. I kept quiet about them and didn't tell anyone. Realistically, I should have phoned the companies to explain my situation, but I didn't have a clue what to tell them. I know they would have preferred some offer of payment rather than nothing, but I didn't have anything available to offer.

After a couple of weeks, a job eventually came my way, but like before, it was a recruitment company, and the job was working at a distribution centre in Magor. It was night work carrying out order picking, which didn't sound too bad. Because my car still wasn't fixed, I had no choice but to cycle there. It was only 10 miles each way, but really, it was the last thing I wanted to be doing with a night of work ahead of me. It was still work though, so I knew I had to give it a shot.

The pay was poor and based on a zero hours contract, meaning I was barely getting 18 hours a week, which could drop without warning.

My luck got even worse when, just a few weeks after starting and just before leaving for work, there was a knock on the front door. It was a chap from TV Licensing, and Selina had only gone and let him in. He told her the premises were unlicensed and that a report would be written up. She didn't know at the time, but I had cancelled the TV licence a few weeks before, along with the direct debits. It might only have been £20 a month, but with no income, it was costing me double that in bank charges. I explained to him why I had cancelled the payment and said I was going to set up a new payment plan online. Straight after he left, I set up the plan online.

I was in a pretty shit situation. Although I was working, my income was still less than my outgoings, and because I received a military pension I wasnt entitled to any other benefits to top up either. I was just using my pension to cover the rent.

Still, the bills flooded through the door. This time, there were disconnection notices. I was really starting to worry now, and the pressure of the situation meant that Selina and I were arguing more. I could have resolved this by talking to my father, but I was angry and far too stubborn, so it was a relief when I finally got a bit of good news.

During the 12 weeks I'd been on the job, I was nominated by the picking management as one of the most hard working and fastest pickers, and with a handful of others I was offered a 6 month fixed term contract. This was good as I was now guaranteed at least 30 hours a week and an increase in pay.

As great as this was, I couldn't shake the feeling that something was bound to go wrong, and it did. Only 3 days into my new contract, I ended up housebound for a week on sick leave with no pay after bursting a blood vessel on my wrist. This was all I needed.

For the first time in my life, I started to suffer from physical anxiety symptoms. I was lying in bed one night, and my face was on fire. You could've cooked bacon on it, It was that hot. I also started to suffer from facial tingling and brain zaps, the latter feeling like an electric bolt to the face. It was really quite scary. As well as this, I suffered with constant stomach problems and was always in some sort of pain.

Leaving for work one evening I'd gone about a mile up the road when my phone rang. It was Selina telling me I needed to come back urgently. I just thought, what the hell now.

It was evident what the problem was as soon as I walked through the door. A bailiff was sitting on our sofa. He informed me that he had come for non-payment of council tax. I felt sick to the core and a bit angry.

Selina and the children sat on the sofa as he began to do an inventory of our goods. He noted the TV and DVD player, our laptop, plus a shit load of other things. He said I could set up a payment plan to clear the arrears but would need to make a payment of £100 today. Fucking hell, I only had £110 in my account, but I knew I had little choice but to pay him.

Once he left, I felt like an outright failure. I was embarrassed and ashamed of myself. What man would put his wife and children in this situation. I hated myself for it, which was made all the worse by the fact that I was trying my best to keep everything afloat. While I was at work, my mind couldn't switch off from the worries at home, and it was affecting my performance. I was still having the hot flushes and brain zaps, but a more troubling problem was my eyes. I began to experience blindness in work, I couldn't see anything. I was under so much emotional stress that my eyes had become extremely sore, constantly burning and watering. The only time I could rest them was on my break. I worked the night shift, so once everyone else went off to the canteen, I sat outside by myself in the dark. It was the only time my eyes could get any rest.

One evening Selina's nan invited us over and offered us £500. A gift to get the MOT passed on the car. I didn't know how to thank her grandparents for their generosity, and I was mortified about taking it. I would never ask anyone for help, I was too proud.

The next day, I got into bed from work at 04:00, absolutely shattered. After a couple of hours of sleep, someone was banging on my front door. I didn't go downstairs; I knew who it was. It was the bailiff. I wasn't in the financial position to fully stick to his payment plan, and now he had come to take further action. He dropped a letter through the door telling me I had 7 days to pay £480 or he would return at 08:00 the following Monday with a locksmith to seize our things. Could it possibly of gotten any worse.

The money that had been put aside for the MOT now had to be used for the bailiff, and to make matters worse, 2 days later, I received a summons for the TV licence. There was a space on the back of the paperwork that I could use to appeal if I believed I had a good enough reason, so I began writing. I explained that I was a former British soldier who'd been injured in a bomb blast. I let them know that I was receiving a war disability pension, and due to unfortunate circumstances, I was going through a period of stress and financial difficulty. I also made a point of saying that

I planned to never let this happen again and that since issuing the summons, I had purchased a valid TV licence.

After a few weeks, I received their verdict. Hello Mr Spencer, Here is a £350 fine for you to pay. Your payment card will follow shortly. I was extremely pissed off with this outcome. I was totally honest and up front with them about my situation, and demonstrated my willingness to comply by sorting out a licence that same day they visited me. I imagine they thought I was giving them a pack of lies, playing the wounded soldier story.

By this point, I had almost had enough. How much more shit could possibly come my way. In spite of what was happening, I still tried to maintain a positive outlook on things. Family life was becoming difficult, and my anxiety problems continued.

Selina and I were at the nursery waiting for the boys when suddenly the nursery teacher came running out from the classroom.

"Can Fabio's mum and dad come with me quickly?" she screamed.

I ran into the classroom to see my little boy lying on the floor, unresponsive and frothing at the mouth. It was too much for Selina, and she burst into tears, running from the room. I wasn't in a much better state, lying there next to my little boy, tears running down my face, and deeply concerned for his wellbeing.

He was having relentless seizures, one after another. His twin brother Nico was also in the classroom with the other children, but mercifully had been taken into the next room. This didn't stop him from developing a stress rash all over his face and arms by way of empathising with Fabio's plight. The ambulance arrived, and during the trip to the Royal Gwent Hospital, he suffered from another 6 seizures. He was quickly put straight onto a life support machine when we reached the hospital.

He was only 2 years old, and to see my son having all these tubes and machines attached to him was breaking me. I was stressed to the max, and having to look after my son meant I wasn't making any money in work and would face even more pressure from the creditors. For the next 4 days, Fabio remained in hospital on the high dependency ward. Selina remained by his side while I looked after Nico back home. What Fabio had suffered from was called a febrile seizure, most likely caused by a high temperature. It was the most terrifying experience and one that I never ever wanted to go through again.

Things continued to deteriorate. The stress I was under resulted in me and Selina separating. We were at each other's throats all the time and said nasty things to each other. Instead of working together as a team, we became the worst enemies.

For me, this was without a shadow of a doubt, the lowest point of my life, I honestly can not put into words how this experience affected me. The car now had an MOT, but only because I had used the money put aside for household bills. At that point, my car was the only thing I had.

Two weeks after Fabio's seizure, I was parked up in my car at the Hanbury Arms pub in Caerleon when I just broke down. My life was in a serious mess; my second marriage was over, I didn't know when I was going to see my children again, and I was homeless with only my car to sleep in. All of my personal belongings were in the boot. Worst of all was that I had nobody to turn to for help. In that moment, I felt desperately unhappy. I didn't know what the hell to do. I couldn't think properly; my head was spinning. I hadn't spoken to a single member of my family in over 9 months, but I knew I needed help.

I walked into Newport City Council Housing Office to register myself as homeless. I sat there, distraught. A member of staff asked me what happened, and I broke down sobbing, I had lost everything and was now living in a car. How could my life have turned out so badly. They couldn't help me. Instead, they handed me a telephone number for a military charity and told me that they hoped they could help. I suddenly felt both angry and sad. Part of the reason I was homeless was due to the stress caused by the bailiffs and their council tax, and yet here I am now, asking for help, and they were turning their backs on me. I left the office fuming. Sod your council tax.

All I wanted was my family back together. How could so much bad luck fall my way. After 2 nights in the car, I took a drive up to Christchurch cemetery. I'm not religious, but I was genuinely on my knees at my mothers' grave, praying for a miracle to save my family. With very little money and no home, I had to do something, I couldn't live in my car forever. Even people I worked with could see that I was barely holding myself together. My work attitude suffered as a result, I was once one of the company's best order pickers, and now I was one of their worst.

I contacted my father and also went to visit my nan. I never liked to ask for money, but if I were to get my family back, it was the only choice I had. I explained my situation, and my nan agreed to help me. We ran through a list of the debts I had, and she gave me over £2000 in cash, I couldn't thank her enough. Yes, it was humiliating and hurt my pride, but my family is what I needed, and that was the most important thing to me. The money helped no end, and I soon had all the bills back on track and was living back home with my wife and children.

I was so happy to have sorted things out, but something had changed in me. During the struggles in the preceding 9 months, I felt like a piece of me had died. A bit like when a boxer loses his hunger to fight, this was now happening to me. I had lost my fire in my belly. When I got back to the gym, I couldn't find any motivation to train. I used to undertake 3-hour treadmill sessions and 1000 rep workouts with maximum dedication and effort. Now, after just 10 minutes on the treadmill, I would hit the stop button. I was giving up on a regular basis, and I couldn't figure out why.

OVER THE NEXT few weeks, family life resumed its normality, and my anxiety symptoms started to ease. One early evening, while Selina was at work, several images started coming through Facebook messenger. They were from my old military friend Mike England.

The images were from the day of the suicide bombings. There were lots of them and I never even knew they existed. There were images of the bombers trucks and also a large number of the carnage that followed. It brought back a lot of bad memories, but it also stirred up something inside me. I remembered what that woman had said to me that Saturday night in Bolero's Bar those years before.

This was all the motivation I needed. I thought a picture paints a thousand words.

The following day, while the twins were at nursery, I asked the receptionist if I could use one of the laptops, and it wasn't a problem. I still didn't have a clue about how to write a book or even where to start. I chose the day of the suicide bombings. It might have been sort of the middle of my story, but it had a massive impact. For about an hour, I typed away while Selina was chatting behind me over a coffee with the other mothers. She turned to me and said, "What are you doing there?"

I replied, "I'm writing a book."

I just heard her giggle.

Every day, while the twins were in nursery, I'd use those few hours to do a little bit of work on the book. I soon brought myself a tablet so I could do some work on it at home and also thought about a good title. It had to be gripping.

I came up with – The battle within, a soldier's story.

Soon after, I started a Facebook page of the same name and invited as many people as possible to tell them about my upcoming book. I had only written a few dozen pages, and it looked a mess. There was no doubt a lot of editing would need to be done, but that could wait. I just knew I needed to keep writing little bits here and there.

When I wasn't in work or writing the book, I got myself back in the gym as I planned for another endurance event.

Chapter 16

Lost in the Beacons

THE NEXT CHALLENGE would be tough. 70 miles in total. The plan was to not only walk the Taff Trail but also the infamous fan dance on route.

The fan dance is a 24km route that's used on the British Army's Special Forces selection as a benchmark for fitness. The route starts in the heart of the Brecon Beacons at the Storey Arms on the A470, then climbs over Pen Y Fan, around a mountain called Cribyn and down a roman road to Torpantau car park, and then back again. The route is notoriously challenging, and as I planned the 55 mile Taff Trail into the mix, this wasn't going to be easy.

I would be doing this for five different military charities. Talking 2 Minds, Combat Stress, Scotty's Little Soldiers, Help4Heroes, and finally Soldiers Off The Streets.

Two veteran's that I had also served with volunteered to take part with me. Eddie served in the support company's mortar platoon with myself, while Ben served in a different company.

The plan was that the lads would travel down, and we would start Friday evening on the 5th December at 8pm. After meeting the lads at Newport railway station and bringing them back to my home. We had a bit of a catch-up on old times as I hadn't seen them in years. It also gave us some time to check our kit and refuel before my father would come to pick us up and take us to Brecon. On the way up to Brecon, myself and Eddie were full of energy and raring to go while Ben slept the way up. At 8p.m, the three of us stood outside Brecon theatre and about to start this distance challenge and hopefully raise some funds for some military charities. The weather was dry but cold as you would expect that time of year.

We set off, and everything was going well. After a couple of hours, we reached the Talybont reservoir, and next was the long uphill stretch to Torpantau. It soon became clear that Ben was struggling a little. Not to worrying, but I slowed the pace a bit. It wasn't a race, after all.

The snow had settled at Torpantau and was slippery underfoot. We now had about 4 or so miles till we got to pen y fan. As we made our way up the snowy roman road, Ben continued to show signs of struggling. He stuck with it, and we eventually made it to the bottom of the Jacobs ladder. It was now half one in the morning, and the weather was dire. Plenty of snow had made the journey up to this point extra work, but we only had about half a mile to climb to the top, and then we would be on the return leg.

Due to the appalling weather conditions and Ben struggling, there was no chance of making it to Story Arms and back, so I said we should just climb to the top.

I recommend we leave the rucksacks at the bottom and climb clean to make the journey a bit easier. I put a cyalume stick on the bags so we could see them on the return, and with an emergency shelter and mobile phone, we set off up Jacobs ladder. It might of only been half a mile but it was hard work with the snow and wind. Visibility was down to just a couple of metres. However, at 2am the three of us safely made it to the top and had time for a quick selfie. We had covered the 15 miles in 6 hours which wasn't bad going, and Ben seemed to bounce back to life. Just back down to Torpantau and we could continue our journey on the Taff trail.

We were making our way towards the Pontsticill reservoir when we had a quick admin stop. Eddie was doing fine and put on some fresh socks while Ben had fallen asleep within a minute or so.

I said, "Come on, Ben. You can't sleep, it's too cold and we have to keep moving."

He just said, "No, I want to sleep."

Along with Eddie, I picked him up, and we got him moving once again. Next minute he's saying I need a fag. I said "Mate, it's half three in the morning and we are in the middle of the Brecon beacons. There isn't a shop for miles."

About 10 minutes later, we see a car driving towards us. Ben starts flagging the driver down and as the car passes he starts running down the road as the driver slows for him.

I just looked at Eddie and said, "What the hell is he doing?"

Ben gets in the car with the driver, and they turn around and come back up the road towards us. The car stops, and the window opens. Ben says, "He is going to drop me off at a shop for fags. I will meet you at the end of this road."

I said, "Wait." But they just drive off.

Eddie starts ringing his mobile, but it's turned off. All we could do was continue to the end of the road and hope he's there. He wasn't.

I had a quick look around the area, and there was no sign of him. Still no answer on his phone. I was beginning to panic. I was concerned that he might have just fallen asleep somewhere, and with the weather below zero, he wouldn't have been in a good way.

I also had the responsibility of his welfare as it was myself that organised the challenge. My mind was overthinking the worst. I had no option but to report him as missing. I told the police our location within the Beacons and they turned up within 10 minutes. They asked us some questions before we chucked our rucksacks in the boot of the car and went to search for him. The only comfort was the warmth of the car. It was so nice after a night on the freezing mountain.

We gave a description, and it was sent out across all levels. Over the next couple of hours, we covered many miles in the car, looking through the beacons and throughout Merthyr. The railway station was also checked, but there was no sign of him.

It was now about 8 in the morning, and hours had passed since he jumped in the car. I genuinely believed something bad had happened to him. We were making our way down a narrow street near Cefn-Coed when Eddie shouted "There he is."

It was a stroke of luck. A minute or so either way, and he wouldn't have spotted him. Ben didn't even recognise us and had no recollection of what had happened. The police were understanding and made us aware that the mountain rescue and helicopter were almost ready to be called in. Surprisingly they offered to run us back to Merthyr Station, where we could continue with the challenge.

They must have had a sense of humour. At that point it was the very last thing on my mind. We did take up the offer of a lift to the station though, just to get the train back home. Ben went back home that night while Eddie crashed at mine for the night.

The challenge was a failure, but it could have been much worse. As the donations had been made. I felt I had to fulfil the challenge. Next time, I will do it alone. But for now, I could rest up and enjoy Christmas with Selina and the boys.

Happy times. Selina and the boys.

Chapter 17

Endurance

Friday 9th January, 2015.

This was it. The challenge with Ben and Eddie last month was a failure, but this time I would be going alone. It wasn't going to be easy as the country was being battered by gale force winds. In honesty, I should of postponed the challenge until the weather improved but I had booked time of work and all my kit was sorted. I decided to just go with it.

It was 6:30 in the morning as I stood outside Brecon Theatre, contemplating the task that lay ahead. Despite the fact that the temperature was below zero, I hadn't bothered to put a jacket on. I'd done enough of these walks to know that within 10 minutes of setting off, my body would soon be nicely warmed up. Having a jacket would mean that not long after starting I'd have to stop to take it off, and that would be a waste of time. It might only take a minute, but with 70 miles to cover and only 24 hours in which to do so, every second counted.

I felt confident I wouldn't get lost. Having already walked the trail four times before and the Fan Dance a good number of times, I was well versed on the routes. I would go as fast as my legs carried me. As it was winter, I was going to be limited to about 9 hours of daylight, with the rest of the time spent in almost pitch darkness. I set off at a comfortable pace, and after 2 hours, I made it to Talybont reservoir, only to be met by a bit of a setback once I got there. The usual route I took through the woods was out of bounds, so I had to take the road on the other side of the reservoir. To be fair, this route was easier, and I started to wonder why I hadn't used it before. That was until I got to the last half mile. It was almost a vertical climb.

While I was making my way towards Torpantau, the weather hit. The wind was so strong that I could hardly walk properly. I couldn't help but wonder how much worse it was going to be on top of Pen Y Fan. As I was making my way towards Cribyn along the Roman Road, the rain started to pick up. Thankfully, I had gone out to buy some waterproof trousers at the last minute. Nevertheless, if the rain persevered I'd look like a drowned rat by the time I finished.

The weather was now making a climbing the fan unlikely. The wind was battering the hell out of me, and is was struggling to stand up, let alone walk. The visibility was down to only a few metres in any one direction.

I got to Jacob's Ladder, the base of the Fan, and saw a figure walking down the mountain towards me. It was a member of the Brecon Mountain Rescue team. He asked me what I was doing alone on the mountain so I explained that I was undertaking this epic 70-mile trek, and that I needed to climb the Fan to get to the Storey Arms before coming back over again.

He thought I was crazy but agreed it was a hell of a challenge. Before he set off, he warned that despite my best efforts and skills, climbing the fan alone in this weather would be a genuine risk to my life.

After he set off, I thought for a couple of minutes about what he said. Yes, part of the challenge meant climbing the fan, but in this weather, was it really worth the risk? I didn't think so. I took the sensible option and opted not to climb.

Even though I now couldn't make the full 70 miles, I could at least have a good stab at my planned route whilst avoiding the summit. So that's what I did. Apart from the wind and rain that were still causing me problems, I was making good ground and was almost out of the beacons as it was beginning to get dark. Unfortunately I still had over 30 miles to cover and this would be in the dark.

The only real problem I encountered was while walking through a wooded area near Quakers Yard. The path was completely blocked by a shit load of fallen trees, which I assumed must have happened that day from all the gale force winds. With a fence on one side and a steep drop on the other, my only option was to try and climb over the timber wreckage.

While picking my way through the mess, a branch caught my head-torch and pulled it clean off. It hit the floor and knocked itself off. I was cursing. I needed another torch to find the stupid thing, but I didn't have one with me. I was on my hands and knees, rummaging along the ground, trying to find the damn thing. More luck than judgement, I did.

The rest of the walk went by without any more drama, and I stopped for a quick selfie below Castle Coch. I looked terrible. I was soaking wet, cold, blistered, and high as a kite on painkillers.

My selfie was that good at capturing my plight that it would later end up winning the Trail magazine "face of exhaustion" competition. My prize was 4 pairs of super high-quality Darn tough hiking socks.

After a couple more hours of pushing through the pain, I finally made it to Cardiff. It was 04:20, and I had managed to cover a total of 64 miles in a little under 22 hours, bringing in over £1,400 for my chosen charities.

The moment I got home, I wanted a nice hot shower. Standing under the water, I felt the pain hit me. I was aching and sore all over, but the buzz I got from finishing made the whole thing worthwhile.

Only a couple of months after the challenge, I was already considering another one. This one was going to be different.

Former Welsh rugby player turned adventurer Richard Parks undertook the challenge of walking up and down Pen Y Fan non-stop for 24 hours as part of his build-up training for his epic

737 Challenge. I thought I could try the same thing but with a twist. First, I planned to complete the fan dance, and then I would do the 24-hour climb. Of course, I would also be carrying a 35lb rucksack throughout.

I already knew about the SF Experience. It was set up in 2013 by a chap called Jason. A Special Forces veteran in remembrance to 3 soldiers that had died during TA Selection. They ran a number of different events based on the UK Special Forces Selection Course. It gave civilians and military alike a chance to find out what recruits are required to do during a real course. It was ideal timing because in June, they were holding the Fan Dance event. I thought this was perfect, I could do their event first and then go straight into my own 24-hour challenge.

Once again, I started intense training, and this time, I contacted the local newspaper to rouse some publicity for the challenge.

A friend of mine from the military, Lee Umpleby, was keen to take on this special event, which was great as more people meant more sponsorship. But which charities should we fundraise for.

Talking2minds was one we both agreed on, but I also wanted to raise for another. I settled on The Cystic Fibrosis Trust as one of Selina's former school friends had a young daughter named Amy who suffered from cystic fibrosis. She was only 4 years old and also lived in Newport, so it felt right to be supporting a cause so close to home.

With all the previous events behind me, I had good knowledge of what kit and preparation was required for such a feat. The only thing that could possibly let me down was my knee. It was still causing me problems, but I reassured myself that this would be the last challenge, so I would push through if necessary.

Funny that, I'd been saying the same thing since my first Taff Trail walk almost 2 years prior.

The night before the event, I travelled up to Brecon. I wanted to make sure I had the best parking spot right in front of the Storey Arms. As the Fan Dance event was on, the car park would be pretty much full if I left in the morning, and knowing my luck I'd end up half a mile down the road. I needed to be as close to the Storey

Arms as possible because my car was my admin point – full of extra food, water, and other kit should I need it.

While to some degree, it was good to get there early. On the other hand, I was bloody knackered. I arrived around midnight and didn't get any more than 2 hours of sleep. Trying to sleep on the backseat of my car was harder than I had anticipated. Not only was it uncomfortable, but every few minutes, a car would come flying past at 70 mph, rocking my car in their wake. There were a few others in the car park who, like me, had travelled there early, but they were in transit vans and camper vans. They no doubt had a better night's sleep than I did.

At 06:30, I was already frying some bacon for breakfast when Lee turned up, closely followed by Jase and the rest of the SF Experience team. Even though I was tired, I was looking forward to the day ahead. Unlike most people doing the fan dance, I wasn't going all out for time. I just needed to finish it before starting the second part of my challenge. The last thing I needed was to go all out on the fan and then have nothing left in the tank.

Just after 09:00, myself and Lee, along with a few hundred other people, started the infamous 24km route. I felt good. I wasn't going too fast, I just kept to a comfortable pace while stopping to take a few pictures along the route.

Once I hit the halfway point at Torpantau, I stole a quick 5-minute break for a drink and some grub before beginning the return leg. I got back to the Storey Arms in a little over 5 hours and was feeling good. Lee had already finished and was chilling on the grass with a drink.

I grabbed a burger from the van and changed my socks ahead of our 24-hour climb. We didn't set off straight away but instead waited for the final runners to get home and the awards ceremony to finish. It had been over 90 minutes since I had come down from the mountain, and my legs were beginning to tighten up.

We started to head up towards the fan once again, but I couldn't keep up. My knee was fucked. With every step I was taking I could feel the cartilage crunching and grinding inside my joint. For fuck's sake, why now. I was determined to make it back up to the Fan, no matter what. It was a painful climb and seemed to take forever.

At the summit, I had to make a decision. Do I continue and risk permanent knee damage, or call it quits and let my knee heal and live to fight another day. The sensible option would be the latter, but I didn't like to give up. In fact, I hated it. I had put a lot of effort into training and raising funds for the charities, so it was a decision I didn't take lightly.

After talking it over with Lee, we agreed to call off the remainder of the climb. Our intention had been to summit Pen Y Fan up to nine times, and while it's possible, with a 35lb rucksack and a useless knee, it wasn't going to happen that day.

A few weeks after the challenge, I was once again back on my arse after losing my job, and soon found myself struggling with only my service pension to live on. Fortunately, it wasn't long until I found a job working as a drayman for Carlsberg.

The life of a drayman. I've always loved working outdoors regardless of the weather.

I loved it and was getting some good hours in. It felt like life was heading in the right direction for once. I even joined a new gym, although I still wasn't too sure of my knee. I had an X-ray, and everything was as it should be, so I was advised that I needed an MRI scan to check if there was any damage to the cartilage. My days of running over mountains with a heavy rucksack seemed like they were coming to a end.

Ever since I completed the treadmill challenge in DW fitness I often thought about doing another. I really wanted to try and cover 100km in 16 hours, and last time, I had fallen short.

I was now a member of Bannatynes gym. They had recently been refurnished with some high-end Technogym treadmills. This was promising. I sent an email to the gym manager explaining my proposed challenge and the charities involved. I picked the same 5 military charities with the only substitute this time being Pilgrim Bandits instead of Help4Heroes. Two days later, I had a reply… it was a GO.

Even though I wanted to cover 100km, I set myself a 16-hour deadline. Whichever one I reached first, that would be it. This time though, my rucksack would be heavier at 35lb. An increase of 5lb might seem insignificant, but when you multiply that by the time and distance, the extra fatigue becomes very apparent.

Despite the fact that my knee was damaged, it didn't give me any real problems on level ground. I was soon back on the treadmill carrying out some rucksack endurance training. It was nothing like before, just fast 5k and 10k runs. Occasionally, I'd mix it up and train outdoors. I would visit Tredegar House and take part in the Saturday park run. Loaded with my 35lb rucksack, I'd sail around the 5k course in 25 minutes.

I had 3 weeks until challenge day, and I'd decided to do it on a Monday as it was always busiest on Mondays and would help with the boredom. I booked the following day off work too, to give me sufficient time to recover.

While I was at work on the Thursday before the run, I suddenly felt ill. I could do without this now. I took Friday off work in the hope that it would pass and I would be well enough for the run. Did it get better. Like hell, It got worse. I developed a chest infection and laryngitis, and to make things worse, I then lost my voice. I had no choice but to postpone the event.

I re-scheduled the event to be held in 2 weeks' time, again on a Monday and with plenty of time for me to recover. Steph, the gym manager, put together some new posters to advertise the run. I thought, if I'm ill again, then I'm calling it off.

Thankfully, I recovered in full and was all set for the big day. The staff let me into the gym a bit earlier to set up. I had my mobile phone, headphones, and charger, and by the side of the machine, a large box full of supplies. I had 12 bottles of water, 2 cans of Monster Energy drinks, Mars bars, and loads of sweets. It was going to be one hell of a long day.

I had two vouchers that had been donated by the Army Parachute Association to support the event. Each one was worth £50 and could be used towards a solo or tandem skydive at Netheravon Camp. I told management that the first person to complete 2 hours on the treadmill next to me could have them. They said they would inform people of the incentive as they arrived at the club.

Instead of shorts I had decided to wear combat trousers because while they're only slightly warmer, they are a lot less likely to cause chafing which is never a good thing to experience on a long walk or run. The event was due to start at 06:15 and I had just enough time to go to the changing rooms and weigh myself. I would do the same thing once I finished, just to see the before and after difference.

Feeling confident, loaded up my rucksack and dialled 960 minutes – 16 hours – into the machine and hit the start button. The next time the rucksack would be taken off would be at the end.

To cover the full 100km I needed to average around 6.2km per hour which doesn't sound like much, but with the weight I was carrying on my back and the humidity in the gym, it wasn't so easy. I kept to roughly 5.8km per hour.

I passed the 50km point in just over eight and half hours. If I was going to make 100km, then I had a lot of work to do. Physically,

I felt good, and I knew I was capable of running a bit if needed. It's a shame the same couldn't be said for my feet. They were in bits. Every so often, my foot position would change, and I'd end up walking on the blistered area. Before long, that didn't matter, though, as both feet were covered in blisters.

As the hours passed by, the pain in my feet really took effect. I was knocking back painkillers like Smarties but they didn't seem to make any difference, and as a result, my average speed dropped. I tried to work out how many kilometres I was likely to cover in my 16-hour limit, and it looked like I was only going to reach about 90.

The last 2 hours became the longest 120 minutes of my life. I've had walked further distances before but this was the longest without stopping once. My body was in agony, and I couldn't wait to finish. It was now 21:15. Only 1 hour to go, and I still had the skydiving vouchers on me.

A young girl then got on the treadmill next to me. I told her that if she stayed on the machine for 45 minutes, I'd give her the £100 skydiving vouchers. She couldn't believe what I was offering and quietly admitted that she'd never spent longer than 20 minutes on a treadmill before.

I understood this well from my own experience struggling to go past 20 minutes. I said, "Well, just give it a go."

At 22:00 the girl finished her own challenge, and 15 minutes later I finished my own. I handed her the skydive vouchers and she made her way home. I on the other hand was broken. My body was in bits. I didn't quite cover the 100km but still managed 88.2km, and my body felt it. More than 2 marathons in a day while carrying a weighted rucksack. My rucksack had been on my back for over 16 hours, and when I finally took it off it felt like I was floating in a cloud.

Before leaving I jumped on the body mass index machine to see the difference between the start and end. I'd burned over 7500 calories. Lost 3lb in bodyweight and 4% in body fat, but my body was in poor condition. One of the gym's personal trainers carried my rucksack and box to the car for me as my legs had cramped up.

After leaving the gym, I headed straight to McDonalds for a large meal and coke. I needed the calories. I also needed to get some sleep as I had an early start at a garage to fit some VW Transporter seats to help my father out. When I got home I had a quick shower before jumping into bed. My feet were killing me, and I needed painkillers to get to sleep.

The following morning my feet were in bits and they swelled up. I had lost toenails and counted 17 blisters across both feet. On top of that, my back and shoulders had been rubbed raw from the chafing and even my arse had been left bleeding. For a number of nights I needed to soak my feet in warm salt water and use ice to reduce to pain and swelling. The soles of my feet were on fire as if I had walked on fire. It was almost 2 weeks before my feet had fully recovered.

Chapter 18

The battle within

WITH THE TREADMILL challenge out of the way, I continued to push on with writing the battle within. I only had a couple of chapters left to write, and it had taken me almost two years due to losing motivation from time to time. There were many times I came so close to just deleting the lot and moving on, as I just didn't think I would ever see the day the book was printed.

I needed some help if this was ever going to happen. I knew of a former commanding officer of my battalion who had reached the rank of Lieutenant-General. General Jonathon Riley was not only the author of several highly regarded books himself, but he was also the Commanding General of British forces in Iraq during the time I was wounded. So he was someone I could do with some support from.

Through various channels, I got in contact with General Riley to ask if he would kindly take a look over my memoir and, if possible, could write a Foreword. He replied and said he would be interested and could I send a manuscript. Naturally, this was a unedited version. About a week later, I got a reply to say the story is great, but my writing needs a lot of polishing up. This I agreed with.

There was no way I could send a book to print in that state. There was also the book cover and formatting that would need to be worked on. Thankfully Selina's uncle Angelo was a top graphic designer who had worked in Dubai on multi-million-pound projects. He kindly offered to create a book cover and format for free. Angelo worked with Creative designer Sam John and they both created a fantastic cover. Also one of Selina's relatives Lucia D'Onoffio and one of my Facebook friends Rhys Hounsell helped with my book editing.

Over the next few weeks, the book slowly started to come together and I could finally see light at the end of the tunnel. General Riley also sent across his Foreword that would be added to the book. As a kind gesture, he also arranged for a book launch that would take place in the Officer's mess at Maindy barracks in Cardiff.

During my final few months of working on the book I also made contact with some other people whom I decided to invite as special guests to the launch. One of these was a bloke called Matt Johnson. Matt had served as a career officer with the Met police and had been involved in several traumatic events including the murder of PC Yvonne Fletcher and the Baltic Exchange bombing.

These events left Matt suffering from PTSD and ultimately led to him leaving the force. To overcome his struggles he turned to write and he had the gift. His first novel Wicked Game become a best-seller having been published a few weeks before. He also lived just up the road in Abergavenny and was more than happy to attend my book launch.

Another special guest was Dan Biddle. Dan had been the most injured survivor of the 2005 London bombings. He had overcome several challenges in his life following that traumatic day and he understood mental illness well. He would be joined at the book launch by his wife Gemma.

I was at work and on my way to the next beer delivery when the email came through from Angelo.

"There you go."

It was my book. Well, it was my PDF file but it meant the same to me. I opened the file and looked through it. It looked very professional, but only when it goes to print will I know for sure. I knew Angelo would be spot on anyway.

I also made contact with Darren, the owner of Tower print in Caerphilly. I'd been recommended to use Tower print by friend Will Kevans. Will was a veteran of the 1982 Falklands war having served with the Welsh Guards, and he was also an award winning singer, songwriter and cartoonist. He had produced his own book about his experience in the Falklands called My Life in Pieces. Tower print had done a fantastic job of the printing work, and so he also recommended them to me.

I told Darren the book format was in A5 size and to be printed in paperback with full colour. I sent the PDF file, and Darren soon got to work. It was a slightly worrying time as the book launch was just over a week away, and I was going away for a few days with Selina and the boys. I just hoped there wouldn't be any printing problems while I was away.

I had a great time away, but I was keen to get back and focus on the book launch. I gave Darren a ring to find out how things were going, and he had about 10 copies printed as a tester for me to check over. As soon as we got back to Newport, I opened the front door for Selina and the kids and was back out the door before they even had a chance to ask where I was going.

I quickly headed over to see Darren, or rather to see my book. I was like a pig in shit as he handed me a copy of the completed book. From those years back of the woman in Boleros that told me to write it. It was finally done. Although it was unlikely to sell like 50 shades of grey, it didn't matter. It was my memoir, and I was proud of it.

I was more than happy with the work and asked Darren to print 100 copies for the book launch.

Feeling quite dapper as I loaded my books into the car. I had a double check to make sure I hadn't forgotten anything. Especially a pen, I would definitely be needing one of those.

The launch was on Wednesday, 29th June. It also happened to be my wedding anniversary. Early morning my self and Selina popped to Cardiff for some food, a bit of anniversary shopping, and also to grab a new shirt and tie for the evening.

My memoir. The Battle Within, a soldier's story.

We arrived at Maindy barracks and met up with my father. Matt Johnson was inside mixing with some members of family, and he gifted me and Selina with a signed copy of his new book, Wicked Game.

General Riley also provided some Canapés and drinks for everyone. Outside I met up with Dan and his wife. Unfortunately due to Dan's disability, we were unable to get him into the Officer's mess. Despite some of the most intelligent military brains also being on camp, it was something nobody had any idea how to achieve. We decided to do the speech outside. General Riley gave a short introduction before I gave a small talk on my book-writing journey. Then, the fun of the book signings. I managed to shift almost all the copies that evening with other books posted out the days following via social media buyers.

It was a great evening that was shared by everyone.

Soon after, I wanted the book on Amazon, but I hit a problem. My books format size wasn't available in Amazon's printing company, then called Createspace. If I were to get sales, I needed the book on Amazon.

Angelo once again kindly carried out some alterations, and within a few days, I was able to send this across to Createspace for my book to be sold worldwide by Amazon. I also paid a small amount for the book to be converted to Kindle. Although in the long run, I ended up removing it as I didn't think it did the book justice.

While the book was selling ok, I realized it wouldn't continue, and sales would slow down. I would need to spend some time and money on marketing. I spent a fair amount on tailored Facebook ads that would push the book out to those individuals interested in my book genre. I also decided on running several book signings at various locations, so I needed a good setup. I made contact with Darren at Towerprint and asked if he could design a couple of pull-up banners, and this he would sort out for me. A cheap moulded table was brought off Amazon, and I was almost ready to go.

Most Saturdays would now be spent doing signings. One Saturday at a location, I spotted a bloke walking over, and I recognised him. He was the manager who sacked me when I was working at the warehouse in Magor over my poor performance.

He said, "Neil, I haven't come to buy a book as I've already got one, but after reading the book, I didn't realise just how bad you were struggling, and it opened my eyes."

He offered me my job back there and then. I thanked him for his kind gesture but declined as I was already working full time at Carlsberg and flat out on the book. I started getting messages from people saying how the battle within had helped them to motivate themselves and others to seek help for their own mental health struggles. I was all too familiar with the ignorance of many when it came to hidden wounds and disabilities.

On one occasion, I was delivering beer to a pub in Newport. I was in the celler talking to the landlord while carrying out the delivery. He asked me how long I'd worked for them and what I had done before.

I said, "I've been with Carlsberg for over a year, but I'd previously been a soldier when I was younger."

He said, "Why did you leave the Army?"

I replied, "I was blown up by a truck bomb."

He just looked me up and down and said, "Where?, you look fine to me."

I rolled up my sleeve and showed him the large scar running around my forearm. He just said, "Well, you should just count yourself lucky that you didn't lose your arm and been worse off like many others. I wanted to punch the guy. I thought, how would he know that I'd be worse off. From my perspective, while those with missing limbs do have obstacles to overcome, they also had a lot more support. When my arm was ripped open, it took me a considerable amount of time to build up the strength again, and this was mostly due to my stubbornness not to give in. I was roping 120kg beer kegs down cellers day after day, albeit with a hidden arm injury. If I had been doing the job with a prosthetic arm, you'd think I was Superman.

Yet this landlord seemed to think I'd be worse off without my arm. There is so much ignorance around hidden wounds, that it would be deemed that someone with a missing limb is worse off than someone with a limb, but that's not always true. Having limbs are only good when they work. When they don't they are more of a hindrance. In some ways having a missing limb can even be a fast track to success and make a individuals life easier. There are many people that have lost a limb or two and will say it's the best thing that happened to them. You see, it can open doors to huge networks of support and allow a individual to achieve things they wouldn't otherwise get the chance.

Unfortunately people are judged like a book, as in just what they see on the surface. Very few individuals take the time to look into a person's journey to see what they have overcome.

To give you an analogy. Imagine two 40 year old men about the run a marathon for charity. The one man has a prosthetic leg, while the other man has both his legs but is riddled with arthritis. Just running a few hundred metres causes pain and swelling Who is going to get the most support and recognition for finishing the run. It will be the man with the prosthetic leg as it will be deemed that his run harder. In fact they both find it incredibly difficult, but while one man has the support, the other is going alone.

The same applies to mental illness. You never know the depths of someone's struggle as its not visible. While one individual with anxiety can still go about with their daily lives, the other is constantly looking at the rope in the garage.

As for the missing limbs, there are definitely times a individual is far best having them removed. I had recently been to a pub to deliver some beer. I was met at the door by the landlord. He was barely able to walk and clearly in some pain. Both his legs were swollen from the waist down. His legs were covered in bandages, and discoloured where the leg ulcers had leaked through. His feet were black, and his toe nails had almost welded themselves together. This was either the result of diabetes or another condition called CVI or Chronic Venous Insufficiency.

I couldn't help but wonder how much better off this individual would of been without those legs. From my perspective, at least he would get his mobility back. I don't believe that all losses are a loss. Sometimes it's a gain.

In many ways, had I not been wounded and faced my own struggles, I probably would never have written a book, and you the reader wouldn't be reading it, but just a few weeks after the book launch, hidden illness was once again about to hit my family.

Chapter 19

It's cancer

IT WAS ABOUT ten days after my book launch when my father started to act strange.

He came into work and told me he had crunched the front wing of his car on a wall. He wasn't too pleased about it, although it could be repaired. When he did the same to the back wing later that day, I knew something wasn't quite right.

I'd never known him bump his car, and for him to do it twice in a day, I wasn't sure what to make of it. The following morning, he then told me that just after I had left, he had caught his finger on the sewing machine. Thankfully, it wasn't bad.

I couldn't work out what was going on. He was as skilled with his sewing machine as Pablo Picasso was with his brush. Only once had he ever caught his finger under the machine, and that was when he first started out. He would say, "Do it once. You'd never do it again." What he meant by that is the pain it causes, means you are extra careful in future.

It was later in the afternoon when he had a problem when trying to tie his shoelaces that things had to be looked at. I watched on as he tried to tie his shoelace. He started to get annoyed with himself.

He shouted out, "These bastard laces."

His brother Dave came in to see what was going on, and he

decided it was best to take him to the hospital for a check-up. The doctors kept him in overnight for observations, and therefore, Dave and I decided that while he was away, we would give his workshop a once over. I'm a firm believer that if your workspace is tidy, your head will also follow. We started early. Something like 5 am. We spent a solid 10 hours flat out, sorting out rubbish, organising tools, and giving the place some fresh paint. It definitely needed it and was much more welcoming.

Later that day, Dave popped to the hospital to check on him. A couple of hours later, my phone started ringing. It was Dave. He said, "I've got some bad news. Your father's got pneumonia. Unfortunately, they carried out further tests, and they discovered it's cancer."

It was lung cancer that had already spread to his brain. How they didn't pick it up sooner, I didn't know. He had been back and forth to the doctors having check-ups for stomach related issues for some considerable time.

He was released from the hospital later that afternoon, so I popped down to see him. When he saw me, he just broke down. None of us were prepared for this. My father had ready watched my mother battle cancer for 3 years before it had come back terminal and took her life, and he now had a similar tough journey ahead. It was going to be a difficult road ahead, and all we could do was pray that radiotherapy would have some success.

He still had a large backlog at work and many jobs he was only halfway through. He wanted to get as much of it sorted while he still had the ability. I was still working for Carlsberg, but I agreed to help him in work as much as I could.

Obviously, due to the cancer being on his brain and his now reduced cognitive ability. He had his driving licence revoked on medical grounds, so I would have to take him to work every day. To be fair, he seemed healthy, and from an outside perspective, you wouldn't have had any idea he was seriously ill. Again, not all illnesses are clearly visible.

Over the next few weeks, we got through as much of the work as we could and contacted customers and asked them to pick up the work we simply wouldn't have time to do. Some of the customers were understanding, while others weren't. Given the situation, there wasn't much more we could do. It was about a month or so after his diagnosis that his treatment started, but sadly, it all seemed to go rapidly downhill from there. He planned a number of radiotherapy sessions, but after the second, he didn't have the strength to continue. The treatment had well and truly wiped him out.

He was given just months to live. I visited him every other day, and each time, he just looked weaker. A palliative care team was assigned to him, and he wanted to remain at home and declined to go to hospice. It was a Thursday afternoon, and I got a phone call from a family member saying I should go to see my father ASAP as it looked unlikely he would last the weekend. I contacted my boss at work and made it clear I wouldn't be in on Friday as I had to visit my father. The boss was understanding, and I was given as much time off as I needed.

The following day, I woke up nice and early and was planning to drop the kids to school before going to visit him until something else happened. At 7am on the dot, there were a number of very hard knocks on my front door.

I quickly run upstairs to take a look through the bedroom window. Holy shit! I could see a large number of police outside, possibly about 12 to 14, with some armed. I started to panic. I ran back down and opened it before they took the front door clean off the hinges.

"Mr Neil Spencer." Asked the police officer.

"Yes." I replied.

"MOD Police. We have a search warrant for these premises."

Heck! Now I really started to panic. What did they want. My initial thoughts were that I had written something in my book that had broken the Official Secrets Act or something along those lines. I mean, why else would the MOD be here at this time in the morning. Some officers came in while the others remained outside.

An officer asked if I knew anything about a Facebook comment. I relaxed a bit as it all started to make sense. About two months prior, a former SAS soldier I knew who runs a close protection company asked if anyone had any old military kit he could use for training demonstrations, etc. As a bit of old military banter, I said yes. I've got a few hundred rounds of 5.56mm ammo. Several hand grenades, some Claymores and also a Law 94. That's a light anti-tank weapon. It appears some of those keywords got picked up by the security services, and the MOD was sent to investigate. Basically, they just came to get their military kit back.

Bomb squad, I was told, were on standby within the vicinity as they believed some of the weapons could have taken out half the neighbourhood. Before the search, one of the officers did a walk through the house with a camcorder to cover them for any later damage complaints. It might have been November, but Selina had already put the Christmas tree up, and the family and children's presents were neatly wrapped up underneath and with some others put under the stairs.

Selina told one of the officers that they could search anywhere, but don't dare touch the presents. Selina gets very protective of the tree, and god forbid anyone touch it or the presents, search warrant or not.

While I was sitting on the sofa. Selina looked across at me with those eyes. She said, "you dickhead. I told you not to post shit on Facebook." The search team spent about an hour going through every possible hiding place, and while I knew I had no military weapons and I hadn't done anything wrong. My worry was that I would be taken into custody for questioning, and my father would have passed by the time I got out. To miss my father's death over a Facebook prank would have been a massive hit.

Thankfully, I wasn't, and about 2 hours after they arrived, they could see it was just a bit of old military banter that was taken a step too far. They gave me a copy of the search warrant before making their way back to Bristol.

Finally after the panic of the past 2 hours I could visit the old man. Although he was very weak, I could see the smile on his face when I told him the drama that had unfolded that morning.

It would be the last time I would see him smile as he would soon be on powerful medication. I spent most of the weekend at his bedside, alternating with other family members, so he was never alone. It was now early Monday morning, and I was sitting in my car outside Greggs with a bacon roll getting ready for another day. Little was I aware of just how much time he had left.

At the house, there was just my grandmother, my sister and her husband, my father's brother Dave, and a member of the end of life team. After sitting with him for about half an hour, I had just gone to sit in the living room with a coffee when I was called back in. It was a very strange experience. My father's eyes had opened, and it was as if he was looking at something in the far distance. I was holding his hand, and my sister was on the other side of the bed as we now faced what would be the last few minutes.

It was definitely the most emotional experience I've ever faced as I watched my father's breathing slow down and eventually stop over the course of a few minutes. My mother's death had also been emotional, but as I still had my father back then, it was far easier to move on. With both parents now gone, I really felt alone in the world.

Dad's death hit me hard, really hard. There were times when I couldn't stand to talk to him, and no doubt the feeling was mutual. But I was very much like him-stubborn. The day after his death, I went to his workshop. A place I had worked alongside him on and off for many years. I made myself a cup of coffee and had a sit down at his sewing machine for a few moments.

Looking around, all his upholstery tools and materials were left as they were when he last used them. I turned on his Singer sewing machine, and the motor started to wind up. Just like a certain song can you back to a memorable time, this sewing machine was no different. He had this Singer 211 machine for well over 30 years and even as a small boy I would help my father by supporting the weight of some of the fabrics he would be sewing. Boat canopies for example. I grabbed a bit of leather off the floor and put it under the machine and run a few stitches through it. It would be the last time I would hear that familiar sound now that he was gone.

FAMILY MEMBERS HELPED with the funeral arrangements, and as well as being a Pallbearer, I would also write a eulogy to read out at the service. The funeral would take place one again at St John's in Maindee. The service was amazing but I was a little disappointed at the turnout. My father was a good man who was always willing to help others and had many friends and acquaintances that he had built up over the years in his personal and business life. It was a shame that so many of them failed to turn up to pay some respects. I guess that life for you.

A few days after the funeral, I took my car to his workshop to give it a clean, just like the old times. I'd just given it a wash, and it was now parked outside the garage doors for the vacuum. I was giving the drivers footwell a clean when I picked up something in my peripheral vision. This human shaped shadow stood within the workshop about 15 ft away. I quickly turned around, and there was nothing. Was it just my imagination, or was it my father just keeping an eye on me. It damn well seemed that way.

In the weeks following the funeral, I started to drink heavily again. No where near as much as did after my break-up from Maria, but still far more than I should have been. I was still working as a drayman, but Carlsberg were going to start disbanding their drayman delivery service. As I was only with an agency, I would have to find another job.

I got wind that drayman jobs were available at Kuehne & Nagel drinks logistics in Avonmouth. With the years of experience with Carlsberg, I sent a quick email across to the depot manager.

He replied an hour later. "You can start next week." This was brilliant. I now had a permanent contract and a decent income. Being a drayman was not a job for those afraid of some hard physical graft or working out in the elements. It was a job that either makes you or breaks you. Many start and quit within a month, while others will continue to grind away for many years. It was a job that I loved.

After a few months with the company, the depot manager said he was going to nominate me for the Ex Forces In Business Awards.

It was a few months later when I received an email saying I had been shortlisted as a finalist in the Inspiration of the Year category. The awards were to take place in London in a couple of months' time. The venue was the Hilton on Park Lane with the main event taking place in the Grand ballroom.

I soon cut back on the alcohol as my health worries about liver damage came flooding back. I was once again back at the doctor asking for a liver function test. A few days later I received a phone call about my results. She said, "Neil, all normal apart from elevated bilirubin. Most likely Gilbert's syndrome."

Gilbert's syndrome. What the heck is that. I quickly typed it into Google. Gilbert's syndrome is a genetic liver disorder where, due to a faulty gene, the liver doesn't process bilirubin as it should. Many of the symptoms include mild jaundice and stomach problems, but it's not related to serous liver disorders like cirrhosis.

I went back to see the doctor to discuss my findings. When I asked to look back through all my previous tests going back over 10 years, the results were all the same, elevated bilirubin. I'm not sure why it took so long for them to discover this, but at least I now had an answer for my jaundice, fatigue and constant stomach problems. It was just a faulty gene and not caused by the years of heavy drinking.

The day of the business awards arrived. I hired a tuxedo for the occasion, and it would be the first time I'd ever worn one. Selina and I decided to set off early and do some sightseeing before the event. I had been to London once before during the fire strikes, but that was business, this was for pleasure. We had a visit to Buckingham Palace and also the outstanding department store that is Selfridges.

The awards evening was fantastic with fine dining and endless bottles of champagne on offer. It wasn't the sort of dining I was used too, but for one night I was going to make the most of it.. The Grand ballroom was packed full of military veterans from all different regiments and units that had now excelled in their civilian careers. Although I didn't win any award on the night, it really didn't matter. It was a night away in London with Selina and a great experience I will remember for some time.

It was a couple of weeks later that I had another strange event take place. I wasn't feeling too good. I was still trying to get over my father's death, I had a few other worries going on and I had a really heavy and long day ahead in work. I just I didn't want to in. I pulled into the car park at 5 a.m, and there wasn't a sole in sight. I just sat in my car for a few minutes deep in thought about the shitty day ahead when the most amazing thing happened.

I'm suddenly overwhelmed by this very strong smell of cigarette smoke that seemed to have filled the car. It was so strong that I could taste the ash in the back of my throat. I immediately think of my father who had been a chain smoker. It was as if he was sitting next to me just puffin away. Afterwards, my day didn't seem as bad.

Chapter 20

The psychic medium

MY JOURNEY OVER the years had definitely been full of paranormal events, and I came close to writing about my experiences in the battle within. As the book was nonfiction, I did wonder how the book would be accepted when mentioning the paranormal world.

It was a couple of years later when I came across another book. The psychic soldier by Bob Curry that I considered mentioning my own experiences in a later edition.

You see, Bob was no ordinary soldier. A veteran of the 22nd Special Air Service. (SAS) Bob had served in many operations, including the Falklands war and also the 1980 Iranian embassy siege, where he earned the nickname back door Bob for smashing his way in with a sledgehammer. But during his life, he felt he had been nurturing another special gift. That of being a psychic medium.

I was fascinated by his journey and his own paranormal events that it inspired me to share my own experiences. So, after experiencing so many of my own paranormal events over the years. I decided to pay a visit to a psychic medium. It was something I had wanted to do for a long time. I had faced all the usual scepticism from the non-believers who claimed they were just conning the weak and those looking for signs from past loved ones.

While I have no doubt that there are con-artists about, I don't believe they are all out to rip people off.

Before I went to see the medium, I learned as much as I could about them and the many tactics they use. A common one is something called cold reading. It's where they throw out let's say, a dozen common names, and they look for your response.

It's highly likely that one of the names you would be able to relate to, and that's where they reel you in like a fish on a hook. They will then use this to build your confidence in them, and then, unfortunately, you will be the one giving the medium the answers and not the other way around.

So I did my bit of research and found there is a way of possibly avoiding the dodgy ones, and that's to find one that has studied at the Arthur Findlay College in Stansted. The college is world renowned for courses in Mediumship and Psychic studies, and it's a place where you will be taught to build on your abilities by world renowned members in the field.

I had been recommended one by a friend who had positive feedback and checked her out. Her profile said she had studied at the college and was less than 5 miles away, so I made a phone call and booked an appointment.

Her name was Jeanette Guerra.

On the day of the reading, I was sitting in my car outside, not quite sure what to expect. I was a little apprehensive but excited at the same time.

I wasn't a full-on diehard believer, but I hardly a sceptic either. I decided to try and play it cool and not fall into the trap of cold reading. I thought that if she said a name I knew, I would pretend I don't have anyone with that name. Well, that was my plan anyway.

Jeanette met me at the doorway and said she felt a lot of energy around me.

As I made my way into her house, she turned to me and said, "So who has a stomach problem?"

Urh, I thought how she would know that. I was already gripped. I said, "Well I do."

She said, "OK."

I soon remembered that my father had also been riddled with constant stomach problems. It was so bad he wore holes in his shirt from the rubbing.

Jeanette led me into the kitchen where the reading would take place. I was half expecting a dark room with some magic ball like a scene with Whoopi Goldberg in Ghost. It was nothing of the sort. There was just a candle burning and a water fountain, and that was it.

"Take a seat, and relax." She said.

The next question Jeanette asked was, "Who feels like they are going to die young?"

I said, "I do."

For many years, I felt that I wouldn't live much past 40, and now Jeanette was picking up on that. It gave me Goosebumps.

Jeanette said, "Well I don't see that happening, so perhaps I'm just picking up your worries."

Jeanette then moves to another question for me, and this was a biggie.

She said, "I'm seeing a wedding and someone that couldn't attend due to a sudden illness. I'm getting the feeling that it all happened so fast."

I replied, "It could only be my mother. Her hips had snapped just 10 days before my wedding. Her cancer had come back incurable." I had no idea how she would have known any of this. She was either genuinely interactive with my mother or it was an amazing coincidence.

Jeanette then starts saying some names, all of which were the names of immediate family members, although she didn't mention the names of my parents. The next question she said was, "I'm seeing a connection with George Street Bridge and also the docks. Does this mean anything to you?"

I said, "Well, yes. The place I first lived at literally backed on to George Street Bridge, and as for the Docks. My father had a business at Jack's pill. That was very close to it."

Jeanette was just making some notes while she was asking the questions and said at the end you could take it with you.

The sign from above. The smudge mark from the doves impact on the patio doors.

The next question was another shocker. She said, "I'm seeing a connection with a farm and the cwmbran area. Do you have any connection with this?"

I said, "Definitely. My father ran his car upholstery business from a farm in Ponthir from 1990 until he passed in 2016. This is just outside cwmbran."

Over the next hour, Jeanette went into more detail.

She said, "Neil, you have 2 spirits that are always attached to you. A young man called Stephen, who hung himself and a baby."

She said, "They're always with you."

It was supposed to be just an hour's reading, but I ended up staying there for 3 hours.

Towards the end, I told Jeanette about many of my own paranormal experiences I'd faced over the years. I also showed her a picture of the white dove that hit the patio doors shortly before my mother died.

I didn't tell her it was a dove. I just asked her what she made of it. Jeanette said, "It looks like a DOG."

I asked what breed of dog, and she replied, "An English springer spaniel."

I said, When I was about 14, my parents got me an English

Springer Spaniel, called Jessie, and the dog was forever playing in that garden."

My reading with Jeanette was remarkable, and although I had no solid proof, there was something special about the whole experience and how she would mention so many events and locations that are personal to me. In the year following my reading with Jeanette, a few more strange events took place. The first one some would call a visitation dream.

It had been 3 years since my father had passed and my grandmother had passed just a few months before. This was a dream like none I had ever experienced before.

I was at my grandmother's house. I can remember moving throughout the house and it was immaculately clean like it used to be. The TV was on, and there was family photos on the wall and on the sideboard. I was stood in front of fireplace with the heat on the back of my legs. My father was sitting on the sofa with a glass of whiskey in his hand, and a cigarette in the other much like he used too. My grandmother was standing to the side of me.

There was a conversation taking place and they were talking about me, but I can't remember what it was about.

What was most bizarre was how amazingly well they both looked. Neither of them looked anything like the age or condition they were when they passed away. My father was only 58 when he passed but he looked like a man in his 80s during his last stages of the illness. In this dream he looked like neither. He could of passed of as a man in his late 40s. It wasn't like a dream at all. They seemed so real as if I could touch them.

My other experience was similar, although I wasn't asleep. I had just closed my eyes and within a few seconds there was a huge flash, and this was followed by what seemed like a old cine film that started playing.

This face of a man quickly came into view, before another image of a black cat. After a few moments later it changed to an ape. It was all very strange, and a few days later it happened again. This time there was a flash, but it wasn't like a film, but instead like a tunnel. It was as if I was looking through a pipe at something in the far distance. It was a man in his 60s with dark hair. I knew I wasn't asleep, as I could of opened my eyes, but I knew the image would of disappeared. Instead I kept looking at it, and it was coming into focus. The man didn't look like anyone I knew but the detail was surreal.

I had experienced so many strange events over the years, but still I thought it could just be my imagination. That was until a neighbour was present during one of them. It was during the summer. There wasn't the slightest breeze, and I was sitting outside my house on the grass and talking to my neighbour who was standing about 5 metres away from me. My neighbour, a nurse at the local hospital was telling me about how her husbands university course was coming along when the strange event happened.

I see something in the corner of my eye leaving my house and walk behind me. Thinking its Selina. I quickly looked over my right and left shoulder but there was nothing there.

My neighbour at this point says, "What the hell just went past you?"

This was all the evidence I needed. I didn't mention anything going past me, and from my perspective it could of easily been a wasp or something similar. When I asked her what it looked like, she couldn't explain what she had seen but it was something.

Something had definitely passed behind me that day. I couldn't see anything other than the glimpse in the corner of my that soon vanished.

Chapter 21

OCD

AFTER STRUGGLING ON for many years with my mental health issues, I contacted a local organisation for some support. After sending off my military details and GP information, I soon had a letter back to attend some treatment sessions. These sessions would be once a week at St Cadocs, in Cearleon. The treatment was being provided by NHS veterans Wales service.

I couldn't wait to start and made a point to myself that I wouldn't hold anything back. I will discuss all my worries no matter how embarrassing they might be.

The therapist was brilliant. After discussing my life story and the many issues I was living with, it soon became apparent that I have OCD or Obsessive compulsive disorder and had been suffering from it since early childhood.

I never even thought about it before, and I believe this is due to the huge misconception about what OCD really is. I think if you asked a general member of the public to sum up their idea of OCD, they would probably say it's someone that has all their clothes in colour order, and everything in the house must be immaculate. While this is true to a certain extent, it is far more debilitating and covers a much wider range than you'd imagine.

During my therapy sessions, we looked back and could see this

OCD pattern that had followed me through the years. From my time as a young boy who couldn't get into bed unless I carried out my ritual to perfection, though to the horrible intrusive thoughts I had about my mother in the family room. Throughout my life every theme of intrusive thought has plagued my mind at some point, and while many have been short-lived, others continue to grind me down today.

One of these themes is ROCD or Relationship OCD. Looking back over the years, I could see this was the reason I ended my first marriage. There was a time when I couldn't be around attractive women. It could be a place of work, the gym and even the supermarket. Just noticing a very attractive women would cause me to question my own relationship.

I somehow believed that once I got married, I would no longer find the opposite sex attractive, and if I did find another women attractive, then I would believe I was in the wrong relationship. Looking back now, I can see how bonkers that seems but that's how my brain is wired.

As with all my other OCD themes, the way I would deal with it was avoidance. That time, I was working in security and believed my ears and nose were growing, and would have to remove the mirrors, to the time with the relationship OCD and seeing an attractive woman. I would avoid making eye contact as much as I could. I would soon learn that it had the opposite effect. The more I tried to avoid a thought or ritual, the more powerful it would become.

Ever since I was a young boy, I'd always been a very deep thinker. If there was something to be found, I wouldn't give up until I found it, regardless of how long it took. That's just being obsessive after all. My mind is either best friend or my very worst enemy. There are times when it's carried me over the mountains alone in harsh weather or hours plodding along on a treadmill, to those moments I can't even leave the house as my negative thoughts are just to damn strong.

My therapist told me to think of my thoughts like driftwood.

He said, "We have thousands of thoughts every day and we can't control them all. So just imagine yourself sitting on the side of a river watching the driftwood float by. You see it come into view and then soon disappears. Your thoughts are no different. When a thought pops up, Just let it go."

That made a lot of sense. I always tried to own a thought. I needed to understand it. Instead it's caused me a lot of suffering. These days I just let it go and so far its helped a lot.

While I've always had these intrusive thoughts. The other side aspects of OCD have also caused me many problems. There was a time when Selina asked me paint a small feature wall while she was in work. When she came home she was shocked to discover that I hadn't just painted the feature wall, but every other wall too. I just got carried away. Once I get into the mind-set, I end up going down a rabbit hole and struggling to get out. I've no doubt it's also one of the reasons I've struggled with alcohol over the years, and also my Obsessive worries about my physical health.

Not so long back, I was at a party and talking to some friends, and I told them that even drinking just 2 pints of lager a day could make you a alcoholic. They just laughed and said I was talking nonsense. Unfortunately, they didn't quite understand what I meant.

You see, most people think a alcoholic is someone who grabs the bottle of vodka first thing in the morning to have with some cereal. While this definitely happens, there are those who are called a high functioning alcoholic. An individual who, despite having a alcohol addiction, can continue to be independent. They can go to work, the gym, and even cook and clean. I would consider myself as one of those, albeit it's more under control these days.

When I say that 2 pints can make you a alcoholic, it's not about how much you drink, but rather your dependency on it. If you need those 2 pints a day and really cant go without, you could indeed be considered alcohol dependent. But im also a realist. I'm fully aware that 2 pints of lager a day is not likely to cause any long-term health problems, as long as it stays that way.

Unfortunately for many, including myself, it doesn't often end up that way. Before long, that single glass of wine at the end of a busy day becomes 2 glasses, and then it's a bottle of wine or 2 every night.

My alcohol units would start creeping up over time. While I might of started off with a double or two in the evening. Before long it was half a bottle, sometimes more. I couldn't be content as the alcohol would wear off, so I would need to keep drinking to stay in that mental state.

ALCOHOL IS SUCH a dangerous drug, as with other drugs, but it is also misunderstood. Society is too fast to label alcoholics as lifes wasters and those who don't want to help themselves. In reality, it's often nothing of the sort. Some of the most successful and hardest working individuals have fallen to alcohol abuse. Very often it's down to what I call the ladder of success. Whenever a individual achieves something positive in their life, they take a step up the ladder. As with any ladder, the higher you climb, the longer and harder the fall. It's not so much about how hard you fall, but how well you take the impact.

If you take a look at some of the most successful people that have turned to drink and drugs. More often than not, its because they have fallen of the ladder and it's hit them hard. It could be a marriage breakup or business collapse etc. A individual should always be very careful when climbing the ladder. You never know when a slip might happen, or who's trying to push you off. Hold on tight, and watch your footing.

Somethings to think about.

Remember the power of repetition, especially when it comes to words. I call it the wall effect. For example, if you kick a wall just once, not much will happen, but if you kick it time and time again, the mortar will begin to crack, and eventually the wall will collapse. The same applies to words. If you repeatedly call a child stupid or a failure, they will grow up believing just that.

An obstacle course can teach some valuable life lessons. As a young soldier at Catterick, I once flew around the course and over every obstacle. That was until I reached the 12 ft wall. I was on my own, and I wasn't going any further. Life is full of obstacles. These aren't monkey bars and 12ft walls, but things like divorce, personal injuries and mental health struggles. We can all sail through these obstacles, but you never know when that one obstacle proves to much on your own. Don't be afraid to ask for help. We can all do with a lift up at times.

THERE HAVE BEEN times when I've been very forgetful, clumsy, and not appearing to be switched on. This has given many people the impression of being a bit slow. I say nothing could be further from the truth. To give you an analogy.

Let's say you went out today and purchased the most powerful laptop available. You bring it home and are amazed by its memory and processing ability. But what happens when you start running more and more programs. Some programs will slow down, and others will likely crash. Now, this has nothing to do with the performance of the laptop, but more what you're expecting from it. It's no different from individuals living daily with OCD, anxiety and other mental health issues.

The human brain is also a processing unit, and for those with anxiety disorders, they're are running many programs at once. While some people are just thinking about work and what to have for dinner that evening, those with anxiety are often stuck in a pattern of overthinking many different things at once. They are an overworked processing unit. If they closed a few programs, their performance on the task in hand would be greatly improved. The same goes for the laptop.

DON'T COMPARE YOUR life to others. Stay on your own track. A 22 year old with a degree and a well-paid job doesn't make them more successful than a 50 year old gaining their first GCSE. It's not about the destination but the obstacles you have overcome to get there. Some have been raised in a wealthy home full of love and positively and supported by the bank of mum and dad, while others have been raised in broken homes full of pain and suffering. Unfortunately, these days, people are judged by what they see on the surface and not what's underneath. As I've always said, sometime you're climbing mountains, while others are just climbing hills.

Remember, even Usain bolt wouldn't look so impressive over the 100 metres if his lane was full of hurdles. It still wouldn't make him any less of a champion.

My rock. With my wife Selina who has been at my side through the good and the bad.

About the Author

Neil is a former British infantry soldier, and suicide truck bomb surviver. He Currently works as a drayman and is married with 3 twin boys. He lives in Newport, South Wales.

In memory of my parents, John and Tina who passed well before their time. Although I know they are probably closer now than ever before.

Printed in Great Britain
by Amazon